How To Increase the Value of Your Business Before You Sell... and Make it More Profitable Now!

Lorraine McGregor

Also By Lorraine McGregor

Fast-Track Secrets for Making Your Business Saleable, book and playbook, co-authored with Rob McGregor

Business owners who are committed to making their businesses saleable will benefit from this comprehensive textbook that provides an understanding of the way buyers view their businesses. In addition to supplying this vital perspective, the McGregors offer their proven, four-step system to help owners learn how to attract a premium offer.

The playbook includes exercises that build an owner's Saleability Blueprint. Once the book and playbook are complete, business owners will know what to change inside their businesses to make them saleable, and they will have the blueprint upon which they can create a detailed action plan.

Make Your Business Saleable Resource System

This extensive resource system includes everything business owners need to make their businesses saleable:

- *Fast-Track Secrets for Making Your Business Saleable*, book and playbook.

- *How to Increase the Value of Your Business Before You Sell... and Make it More Profitable Now!*

- Three videos on how to make three critical decisions.

- DVD series of nineteen video interviews that provide business owners and their advisors with the knowledge they need on the journey to becoming saleable.

*For Rob Roy McGregor
who helps me find the words for
what I really mean to say.*

WHAT BUSINESS OWNERS ARE SAYING

"Having owned several businesses over the years, I always wondered why I couldn't get more out of them while I owned them or when I sold them. After reading this amazing book, I now know. The value was always there; I just didn't know how to maximize it. Thanks to the McGregors, now I do. Finally, the definitive answer to the question I always ask about my businesses, "How can I take them to the next level?" If, like me, you want more, then devour this material. It'll change your future!"

James Richardson, President, J2 Investments

"In the midst of the daily battle that comes with owning and operating a business, creating the best and necessary preparation for the owner's inevitable exit may seem like a luxury or may be the last thing on the owner's mind... until it's too late. Lorraine Rieger McGregor has gifted business owners everywhere with a simple, yet thought provoking path to the fulfillment of their highest exit strategy hopes in this book."

David Frank McSpadden, CEO, RethinkAge Institute, LLC, former President and CEO, McSpadden Development Corporation, and author of *Gonna Jump?... Take a Parachute*

"Often when you read a "how-to" book, you are cognizant there is so much more the author is intending to communicate, yet the "how-to" steps are not provided. You feel like you've been handed a full-color, glossy photo of a gorgeous home and told you are expected to go build it from the photo alone. This is not the case with this text. Being a past client of Rob and Lorraine McGregor I felt like I had special insight into their written words as I read their book. The concepts, neatly written in sentences throughout the book, meant so much more to me since I had the immense privilege of being taught and coached by the authors the very nitty-gritty behavioral adjustments required to achieve their book's written concepts. The coaching put the "meat on the bones" so to speak. After reading their published book, I could now appreciate the big picture of what it takes to have a successful business defined by my values, needs, and desires. I was also intrigued to realize the coaching track I was on would help me to not only make my business as profitable as it can be, it would also be the same steps I would need to take to maximize my return if or when I decide to sell my business one day. This book is a must-read, and their coaching far exceeds any professional track I have ever been on. Warning! Only read the book if you desire to rise to your given potential!"

C. Esther De Wolde, CEO, Phantom Mfg., Int'l Ltd.

WHAT THE EXPERTS ARE SAYING

"Every private client advisor (or wealth advisor or relationship manager) should provide their clients who own businesses a copy of this extraordinary book... This book is a fantastic breakthrough resource for preparing to sell your business at maximum value. If your client owns a business, they need to have this book. They will thank you endlessly and never move their wealth to another advisor."

Thomas R. Sweet, Former VP Consumer Marketing, City National Bank, Beverly Hills, CA and Former VP Marketing, Nevada State Bank

"Insightful! What a great roadmap for maximizing the sale of a business. As a business lawyer, I often see overwhelming challenges for business owners who do not prepare for the sale in advance. An ounce of prevention is worth a pound of cure, and there is a ton of information in this book that will help sellers quickly turn their businesses into ones that are saleable. I plan on recommending this book to every client who is thinking about selling a business or even just starting a business and wants to build it right from the start. Not only will it make business owners smarter about selling a business, it will make them smarter about running a business!"

Roger P. Glovsky, Esq. Venture Attorney, Indigo Venture Law Offices and founder of the Seminar, "How to Save Thousands of Dollars on Legal and Professional Fees by Preparing in Advance for the Sale of a Business"

ABOUT THE AUTHOR

Lorraine McGregor is the co-author with her husband and business partner, Rob McGregor, of *Fast-Track Secrets for Making Your Business Saleable*, the first step-by-step manual and workbook on how to make a company worth the value for which the owner wants to sell it. As management consultants, the McGregors coined the term "saleable" and have proven with their own clients that a saleable business is a more profitable business.

Since 1990, Lorraine has helped more than one hundred business owners in a wide variety of industries grow to the next level. She brings clarity to the difficult decisions about where to invest in people, resources, and actions in order to get the desired results.

Lorraine is also the past president of the Vancouver Chapter of the Association for Corporate Growth, the leading mergers and acquisitions association for "Dealmakers," the people who manage the transactions of buying and selling companies. She holds a Masters in Business Administration from Simon Fraser University.

She regularly speaks to the influencers of business owners: their wealth managers, private bankers, accountants, lawyers, and financial planners across North America to help them understand the challenges a business owner faces in making the exit decision.

Lorraine and Rob enjoy sailing their Catalina 34 through the magnificent waters of the islands off the British Columbia and Washington coasts.

DISCLAIMER

The information contained in this document is subject to change without notice, and it represents the current view of the author.

Compliance with all applicable copyright laws is the responsibility of the user. Without limiting the rights under copyright, you may not reproduce any part of this document, store or introduce any content contained herein into a retrieval system, transmit in any form or by any means (electronic, mechanical, photocopying, recording or otherwise), or for any purpose without the express written permission of the author(s). The information contained in this document is proprietary and the exclusive property of the author, except as otherwise indicated.

The information in this document provides content for discussion and general informational purposes only. The author MAKES NO REPRESENTATIONS, WARRANTIES, EXPRESS, IMPLIED OR STATUTORY, REGARDING THE INFORMATION IN THIS DOCUMENT. Nothing in this document constitutes investment, accounting, tax or legal advice. The reader is solely responsible for any use or application of the information or results achieved from the content. The author advises you to seek appropriate investment, accounting, tax, legal, and other professional advice in accordance with your applicable jurisdictions prior to acting or relying on any of the strategies in this book.

The case studies included in this book are based on our client files. Names, numbers, strategies, and defining features have been changed, and some of the characters are composites of several people.

All of the achieved results are factual.

How To Increase the Value of Your Business Before You Sell... and Make it More Profitable Now!

Copyright 2012 by Lorraine McGregor

ISBN: 978-1-61863-621-8

Printed in the United States of America

First Edition Published May 2012

Third Edition Published January 2014
Bookstand Publishing   4001_5

SPIRIT WEST MANAGEMENT, LTD.
718-333 Brooksbank Avenue, Suite 327
North Vancouver, BC Canada V7J 3V8
To Order: www.SpiritWest.com/Products
info@SpiritWest.com

TABLE OF CONTENTS

INTRODUCTION

Many business owners expect to fund their retirement based on the proceeds from the sales of their companies. The ongoing study by Vianello Forensic Consulting,[1] "Marketing Period of Private Sales Transactions," and The American College's State Farm Center for Women and Financial Services[2] both warn against relying on this expectation.

The statistics tell an even more desperate story. Ninety percent of business owners who attempt to sell either fail to find a buyer or, if they do find a willing buyer, then they are unable to close the deal.

Why do so many successful business owners struggle to find buyers? Why do dreams of selling businesses to fund retirement die on boardroom tables?

1. **Successful But Un-Saleable:** Owners are not aware that the typical business, despite being successful for the current owner, is not saleable and, therefore, is not transferrable to a new owner.

2. **No Time to Prepare for Successful Exit:** Owners are not aware that they have to make the company saleable. And so, they are also not aware that it can

---

1 Private Firms Linger Longer on the Selling Block, Business Valuation Update Issue #132-1 September 11, 2013

2 Financial Goals, Concerns, and Actions of Women Business Owners – Focus Retirement Planning February 24, 2012 http://womenscenter.theamericancollege.edu/uploads/documents/Women-Business-Owners-Retirement-Study-022412-v2.pdf

take two to four years to make the changes inside the business that make the company transferrable and saleable.

3. **Circumstances Dictate Exit Dates:** Owners tend to put off the idea of exiting until an external event forces them into looking for a buyer. They then find out, at the worst time, that the company is not saleable. There is now no time available to change the situation.

4. **No Thought of Return on Investment:** Owners tend not to view their businesses as assets that have to be managed in order to get returns on all that they have invested.

5. **Advisors are Not Aware:** Advisors generally don't know that their clients' businesses are not saleable and that there is an actual process to make them saleable. As a result, advisors are not prepared to help a business owner client come to terms with this challenging situation, set an exit date, and make the changes in the business that it needs to become saleable.

Since 1990, my company, Spirit West Management, has helped business owners grow to the next level. During that time, naturally, some clients started to wonder how to spend less time in the business and even how to sell it.

Since 2000, Rob, my partner and husband, and I have worked directly with buyers to understand how they search for acquisitions and what makes them say yes to one out of every one hundred companies they look at.

To help our clients, we took our research on buyers and developed it into a four-step system that shows how to make a business saleable.

Then, a surprising result surfaced. When our clients followed this system, they all received an immediate side benefit: Their companies became more profitable and easier to run.

Most importantly, our clients attracted buyers willing to pay premiums for the rights to acquire their businesses. In fact, some clients doubled the value of their companies within two years of applying our strategies.

Our mission is to share this system that shows how to get similar results with all business owners who want the certainty that they will be able to sell their companies. This outcome is far more preferable than what 90% of those who have tried to sell and failed have experienced – watching their lifework wither away as time goes on and the company does not attract a buyer.

To that end, in this book, we offer business owners and their advisors an introduction to making a business saleable. Your time spent learning the concepts will prepare you to decide whether this direction is the right path to choose.

The concept of becoming saleable is not difficult on the surface, but it is a significant mindset shift. In the following chapters, you will learn how to see your business as buyers do.

Once you have completed this book and decide that setting an exit date is far more important than you first thought, then you will be ready to take on the challenge of making your business saleable.

After you have made this first decision to reposition your company, you will then want to dig into learning how to do it. The Make Your Business Saleable Resource System is a self-guided program that takes you through each of the four steps in deep detail. It includes a playbook of questions that will help you build your customized Saleability Blueprint, which is the plan that reveals what you should change in your business in order to make it saleable.

As you learn more, you also have the guidance of nineteen experts who, through video interviews, provide wisdom and advice on everything, such as what it's like to try to sell a business, how buyers see your company, how and why a bank would finance a management buyout, and how to prepare for sudden wealth. You will also learn how to lead yourself through the change. Yes, change will be your new ally in making your business saleable.

Should you, like many of our clients, decide you want guidance through this journey, our firm offers group mentoring programs. You will join 8-10 other business owners in non-competitive industries and work together with trained facilitators to make your own business saleable. Call us at 206-395-3540 to see if we have a mentoring program in a location convenient to you.

What does it mean to have a Saleable Business? Your company is transferrable, consistently profitable, and ready to or already growing. As a result, you will be able to do any of the following:

1. Get financing for an employee to buy you out.

2. Get financing to help a family member buy you out.

3. Get financing at an agreed upon valuation so you can buy out a business partner.

4. Attract a strategic or private equity buyer.

5. Sell to another entrepreneur.

6. Take on a new business partner who will buy out your shares over time.

7. Sell a minority or majority stake in your business

while retaining some equity to retain a portion of the upside as the company grows under its new owners.

8. Find and hire a general manager who will run the business for you and grow it to the next level until it's ready to sell for your asking price.

What you are about to learn is that there is far more involved in making a company saleable than setting an exit date and hiring a successor. To be ready to sell involves the need to: shift your mindset; deal with emotional and psychological barriers and difficult choices; be willing to change how you lead and how you run your business; and put in place the critical success factors that tell buyers your company is their ideal acquisition.

Let's begin at the beginning in order to clearly see what it means to make your business saleable.

CHAPTER 1

WHAT GOT YOU STARTED? IS IT STILL THERE?

I n this chapter, you will learn:

- What motivates you.

- Why that motivation is key to making your business saleable.

- How business owners determine when to exit.

- Why choosing an exit date is preferable to being forced to exit due to unforeseen circumstances.

I want you to think back for a minute to the time when you started your business, practice, or service. What was your intention in starting your company? Do you remember your passion and excitement for what the future would hold?

Then, as you built your business, what drove you to put in the hours you did, to come up with the solutions to solve the problems, to deal with all the sticky situations and people problems, the rollercoaster economy, and the burden of carrying payroll? What was your big dream? Is it still there, beating a steady drum for you?

You need to be rewarded for all that ingenuity, all those sleepless

7

nights, and all those ridiculous rock-and-a-hard place decisions you've had to make. I know how to help you obtain that reward.

Imagine yourself receiving the biggest check you've ever seen, the return on investment (that's the big reward!) for all that you have built.

All you have to do to get that check is to run your business like an asset that must provide a return on any effort invested. That return is for you, your partners, and your stakeholders. That return is also for the next owner. This is what this book is all about.

In the following chapters, I will reveal to you the secrets that are normally locked away in the minds and playbooks of buyers. I will expose you to the problems that you may not know about that are facing boomer business owners around the world. Their lack of awareness about these barriers is undermining their current and future wealth. Happily, because you are getting this intel early on in your run up to your big exit date, you will be far ahead of the pack.

I am unveiling the entire blueprint right here. These are the milestones that cause your business to become a saleable company. This is the same four-step saleability system that I use with my clients to help them position their companies to be both saleable and more profitable.

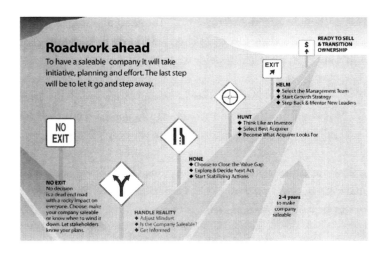

Figure 1 – The Steps to Build a Saleability Blueprint

For every client we work with, we follow the four-step system to help them discover the secret sauce that makes their businesses more profitable, easier to run, and positioned so that the owners can sell them when they want for what they want. The four steps are: 1) Handle Reality; 2) Hone Goals and Decisions; 3) Hunt the Right Acquirer; and 4) Helm the Transition. We will go into each of these four steps in detail in the next few chapters.

You are about to learn how to look at your company in the same way that buyers do. You will understand the red flags that buyers consider, such as profitability leaks (how your company makes and loses money), as well the green light opportunities (for which buyers pay a premium). As a result, you can maximize the return that you will get on the biggest asset you own.

However, before we take you on that journey, you have to know why you would want to go.

What got your company started isn't what keeps you going today. Some owners are locked into their daily routines and obligations. They do not spend their time thinking about and seeing the potential of their futures. When you don't think about what you want, you only get more of what you already have.

What would drive you to exit your business? It's your baby after all. What will motivate you to get off the day-to-day treadmill and really set yourself up for that big payday?

Below are some of the reasons why our clients have chosen to make their companies saleable. Perhaps some of these reasons might be true for you, as well.

1. **Finish the Game:** They have accomplished a lot in their business lives. Selling the business will be like finishing the race, getting the gold, winning the lottery, and especially, as one client said, *"It's the right way to end the story for me and continue the adventure for my employees and customers."*

2. **Get the Reward:** The idea of being given millions for something they created themselves is deeply satisfying and very tantalizing. *"It's hard to believe we started this company on two credit cards and a bold call to a big customer, and now if we sold the business we would be millionaires!"*

3. **Sell Before the "Best Before" Date:** Business partners have watched one another age and have seen their enthusiasm and ability wane over the years. Selling is a way to reinvent themselves before time catches up with them. *"I've watched my partner lose his joy for what we do. I hate seeing how stressed he gets about things that never would have fazed him before. I don't want to end up in the same boat."*

4. **Financial Certainty:** Business life has been a series of ups and downs. All that uncertainty has been

a thrill ride but a little tiresome. There is a huge desire to feel certain that there will be money in the bank to take care of family needs, wants, and freedom. *"There is more to life than running this company. I want the financial freedom to contribute in a new way. I need to refresh my life."*

5. **Win the Race:** Sometimes, it's the chance to trump competitors that drives an owner to sell, especially if the industry is consolidating. Being selected as the key acquisition over other companies is their way of winning the race once and for all. *"I've been watching our competitors shrink and swell for years. I'm not shrinking next time there is a downturn. I'm going to get my exit now."*

6. **Pass the Torch:** As an owner ages and they see the energy and excitement of younger employees, they know that at some point they will lose the spark, the will, and the drive to push the business further. They've chosen to plan for that day in advance so the company doesn't decline under their watch. *"I think we have a lot of bright, eager people here who could lead this business to new heights, and I want to see them put their strengths to work in this company, not leave because I'm not driving the business the way it could be."*

7. **Adapt or Die:** As industries change, companies must adapt or risk being pushed out. The right time to sell is before seismic shifts occur in the marketplace. Smaller companies often don't have the resources to ride out the changes. *"At the size we are, we can't get the economy of scale we need to reduce costs, so we have to grow and adapt, which takes investment. We've got the know-how; now we need the buyer with deep pockets."*

8. **Spouse Says It's Time to Stop:** Often the wife or husband can see changes in the business owner that signify that enough is enough. There are other activities and desires yet to be explored, and the spouse sees that these opportunities will continue to wilt away the longer the owner stays enmeshed in the company. *"My wife and I only see each other when we are on vacation. I see my friends doing some fascinating work on boards or mentoring entrepreneurs or doing projects to help people. Maybe she's right. It's time to find out what else I can do that is satisfying."*

Which one of these reasons for planning an exit date rings a bell for you? Take a moment to write your reason down on a Post-it note. If you don't find a resonator among these reasons for exiting, then write down a list of the possible alternatives that might urge you to seek a buyer.

What is the most powerful motivator behind the reason you selected? Write that down, too, and then put this Post-it note on your computer screen.

Let's continue.

Now, here's a list of reasons – according to business brokers, bankers, lenders, and mergers and acquisitions advisors – that motivate business owners to seek out a buyer:

1. **Divorce:** The judge has ordered the sale of the business, or the financial expectation is to divide the wealth of the business. The owner has no choice but to sell in order to come up with the cash to divide the assets.

2. **Health:** The owner has found that the stress of running the company is a factor in the deterioration of his or her health, and since there is no one who can

take over, the owner must try to sell it.

3.   **Death:** The owner has passed away, leaving the business to the spouse. The spouse is often in the dark as to how the business operates and can only rely on staff to step in and manage the business. If this doesn't work because the owner did not prepare the staff to run the business, the only option left is to try to sell it. Imagine how hard this will be on the surviving spouse.

4.   **Too Tired:** One morning, the owner just wakes up and decides he or she has had enough and doesn't want to run the business anymore. Owners in this situation have lost the "juice" and the passion to continue to deal with the day-to-day crises.

5.   **Partnership Ending:** The owners are fed up with one another and have not been able to reconcile their differences with respect to how the company should operate or be led. One or more want out of the business, so attempting to sell it is their solution.

6.   **Industry Slow Down:** Business has been slow lately, profits are inconsistent, and competition has moved in. The owner wants out before things get any worse.

7.   **Kicking the Tires:** The owner hears that another business owner has just sold their company for a handsome price. On learning about the deal, the owner starts to compare his or her business to the one that just sold and sees a lot of favorable similarities. They turn to a broker to see if they could get a similar deal.

Are you waiting for any of these events to happen to you? All of these reasons for selling have a common theme: They are reactions to external events that leave the owner with limited choices and, in some cases, no choice but to push for any kind of solution to release funds locked away in the business, regardless of the side-effects of such actions.

An owner that has limited choices is at the mercy of the marketplace. But they are really only limited by the amount of care and preparation they have or haven't put in to make the company saleable.

A business broker or mergers and acquisitions advisor can only work with what the business owner has done to prepare the company for attracting a buyer.

Take an honest look at your business situation. Which of these events were you waiting for in order to drive you to an exit decision? Write down your answer.

Should one of these events happen in your life, I would be concerned for you. There is less than a 10% chance that your company is in the shape it needs to be so it can be transferrable. Despite the fact that it is successful for you, it needs to be consistently profitable, and poised for more growth. And these facts need to be obvious to the potential buyer.

Therefore, when one of these events happens to you and you are suddenly forced into needing an exit this year, the broker you choose may or may not accept you as a client. They can't sell an un-saleable business so they are selective. If you are accepted, they will charge you a monthly retainer to help you get your company in order so you can survive the due diligence process and complete a formal valuation.

Even so, let's be perfectly clear: Just because a broker accepts you as a client and you spend $10 to $30,000 a month to put your house in order, do not expect that this effort automatically makes your business saleable or worth what you hope to sell it for. The process of selling your business is not like selling your house.

When selling a business:

- There is no organized, multiple-listing service of buyers and sellers like there is in real estate.

- You can't just "spruce up" the business in a few weeks or months like you can a house and easily attract a buyer. It takes two to four years to make a company attractive (transferrable, worth what you want to sell it for, and positioned for an ideal buyer to gain value by acquiring it).

- People searching for or selling a house often have to be in the new one by a certain date, so time pressures can drive deals. Buyers of businesses search until the fit is right. Time is not of the essence for the buyers like it often is for the sellers of businesses.

What if you don't want to sell it to an external buyer? What if you think your best exit is to sell to your employees or a manager? The reality is that if you need a speedy exit to free up your illiquid assets, then you can't count on this idea to solve your problem.

Employees and managers have been living on a salary. Chances are that they will need financing to buy you out. Management buyout financing requires getting a bank involved. The bank is going to evaluate your business in the same way a buyer would. They will ask, *"Will this business survive and thrive if the owner leaves? Has the owner transferred key relationships to employees who will stay with the company post exit? Does it have consistent cash flow and profitability to pay back the loan and keep growing? Does the manager have the skill and experience to lead the company in the same way or better than the current owner? Is the company ready for more growth? Does it have a strong market niche?"*

Additionally once the financing is in place, your buyout would be staged over as many as five to seven years, depending on the agreed upon price. So, your future fortunes will be tied to the abilities of your manager and employees to achieve the forecasted success in the years to come.

Considering the statistic that 90% of owners fail to find buyers, why would you, an informed owner, do anything other than make your business saleable?

The alternative is to hope that your business will be different. Surely, your business, because of how successful it is, will attract a buyer and get into that 10% club. It might. However, wouldn't you rather know you have done all you can to ensure that your company will be saleable and that you will be able to sign a deal that moves the wealth from inside your company to your personal bank account without damaging the business?

You might imagine what would happen if you'd spent the money on the broker and spent months providing all the information needed for due diligence only to have no buyer emerge. You're ready for that exit. Because of life's circumstances, you need that exit. Yet, it eludes you, and you still have a company to run. What would you do then? It's better to take steps now that will ensure your path never becomes that shaky.

Considering all that you have just learned, when will you get real about your exit?

I want to encourage you, push you, yell from the rooftops, beg you, ask your mother to tell you, and most importantly, influence your spouse and advisor so that whatever you do in the next few years, you:

DESIGN YOUR EXIT ON YOUR TERMS!

- Set your exit date based on what works for you.

- Build your Saleability Blueprint to make your business saleable.

Do this, then you know that your company will continue on into the future, a legacy to all that you have achieved.

Your business will continue to deliver reliable value to customers and suppliers. It will thrive as a great place for your employees to develop their careers and support their families. Your wealth will now be secured – it will be yours to use to finance your next act and your family's future.

If this kind of certainty is what you are looking for, then it's time for you to learn how to see your business the way buyers do.

Imagine having the certainty that you can deliver on that promise you made to yourself and your family of exiting one day.

Imagine the dramatic impact when you attract a buyer who loves everything about what you have built.

Imagine how your life will change when you get that big payday.

Imagine how excited you will feel knowing your employees will enjoy continued success because the new owner of your business cares about driving growth the same way you do.

If your heart just started to beat a little faster, then you're in for a treat and you're in the right place. If it didn't, you really need to keep reading!

In anticipation of the good to come, take a minute now to thank whoever shared this book with you. That person is responsible for setting you on the right track to free your wealth.

You are about to take a fork in the road that many business owners miss. One fork leads to building a saleable business.

THE FORK IN THE ROAD MOMENT

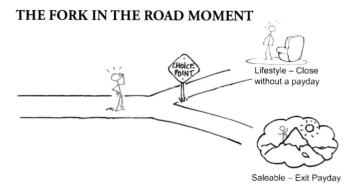

Figure 2 – The Fork in the Road Moment

The other road, the Lifestyle Business, leads to more of what you have today... salary and dividends. Which is fine as long as that is all that you want. What is not good is hoping you will easily sell your business and get a big exit payday worth far more than a salary and dividends, but doing nothing to transform the business so it is saleable which give you the power to achieve that end goal. Are you living on what we call "a diet of hope and promises."

Which future are you aiming for? What are you doing to make it happen?

CHOICE POINT: So, are you going to reinvest in yourself, what you built, and your future and devour this book? Or will you just kind of skim it?

Chapter 1 Summary

Read the bullet points below. If you don't understand why these are the important points, then you might want to re-read this chapter because you need to reset your assumptions about what it takes to sell your business before proceeding to the next chapter.

- 90% of companies today are not operated in a way that makes them saleable: transferrable, consistently profitable, and positioned for growth.

- Discover what will motivate you to sell so that you become intentional in your actions. This is an essential first step and helps you to adjust your mindset about exiting.

- Recognize that you may be motivated by what you don't want, not what you do want. And this thinking habit takes you in the wrong direction.

The choice to make your business saleable creates certainty that you will secure the wealth in your pockets instead of leaving it locked inside your business.

CHAPTER 2

WHAT IT MEANS TO HAVE A SALEABLE COMPANY

In this chapter, we will demystify:

- How conventional wisdom keeps business owners from getting a return on their investment.

- What becoming saleable means by understanding what un-saleable means.

If you are not disturbed already by what you have learned, this next chapter might shake your thinking and sense of security. The idea that you will be able to sell your company when you feel like it is what most business owners rely on as an exit strategy. We call this "Waitingitis."

Let's get down to the root of the problem. There is a pervasive attitude that has invaded the minds of boomer business owners.

Evaluate for yourself if you've got Waitingitis lulling you into a false sense of security. It is the idea that you will be secure in your financial future without doing anything to create that security. It's acting as if everything is going to fall into place and you will exit rich. Your business is as successful as it is because of your efforts. So why would you think your exit would be successful without adequate preparation?

This kind of thinking is ruinous for many people. It's kind of like believing retirement will be taken care of by winning the lottery.

Here's the conventional "wisdom" about what is involved in exiting a business: When you finally feel like exiting or suddenly have to sell or are forced to buy out a partner, then this is what simply has to happen and it can all be taken care of in six to twelve months. This so-called wisdom is tricky in that it involves what appears to be a solid plan:

1. Build a succession plan.

2. Take care of tax issues with the right estate planning.

3. Hire someone to run the business, or put a family member in charge.

4. Audit the financial statements.

5. Call a broker or M&A advisor.

6. Entertain offers.

7. Negotiate the price.

8. Close the deal.

What could possibly be missing from this scenario? This list covers all the important parts: tax, leadership, the sales transaction, and the price. What else is there?

Let's break it down so that the missing elements become clear.

You might have heard from your lawyer, accountant, insurance advisor, wealth manager, or even your neighbor that you need a succession plan. For years, it's been so over-pitched to business owners by the media that the ideas behind it have become empty and meaningless. There doesn't seem to be any immediate payoff to investing precious time and energy into a succession plan now, with an exit so far away, so why bother?

If you knew that the key to claiming your wealth from all that you have built inside your business was spending two to four years making some specific changes inside your business, then you'd probably stop tuning out the succession advice.

So, do you need a succession plan, or do you need more than that?

Well, you need to understand the barriers in the way of you claiming the value – the wealth – you have built up inside your business.

"Succession planning" as used by advisors, is the euphemism for removing those barriers.

It's time to plant a new idea in your mind. A succession plan is necessary, but it only determines how you and your skill set will be replaced when you leave or transition ownership. Don't believe this is the only step that gets you a successful exit. There are four steps that come before the execution of a succession plan.

You can't build a succession plan until you have a blueprint for how your business will become saleable.

A saleable business is structured in a way that appeals to a buyer.

Just like you figured out the equation for your product and service to be the best solution for your ideal target market, you need to figure out what your ideal buyer is looking for. They want an acquisition that meets their needs and is packaged in a way that works for them. When you have their equation figured out, you then know what kind of succession plan the company needs... and this plan dictates your personal succession plan.

Saleable businesses attract buyers looking for what your business can do for their futures. Buyers look for future growth and future cash flow. To be able to grow, they have to be able to capture a bigger share of their own markets or enter into new markets.

For instance, when Amazon bought Zappos, the online shoe retailer, for $1.2 billion, it was already in the online shoe business. Amazon wanted to grow that part of their business and recognized that Zappos had brand recognition and loyalty because it had worked hard at consistently delivering its "secret sauce."

Amazon selected Zappos over all of the other online shoe retailers because it offered growing cash flow, a strong brand to which Zappos clients were devoted, new customers for Amazon's other lines of business, and the opportunity to learn how Zappos' culture supported that customer loyalty (their secret sauce).

Furthermore, amongst those hundreds of online shoe stores that Amazon could have bought, Zappos got the offer because it had built systems that enabled a rewarding customer experience that drove customers back to its site over and over again. Zappos had perfected its secret sauce.

Clearly, Zappos fit with Amazon's strategic growth goals. Your business will need to find the same alignment with an ideal buyer.

The implementation of a plan that amplifies your secret sauce is one of the key ways in which you will increase both your attractiveness to a buyer and also the Multiple, which you will learn about shortly.

Often, buyers need to add products or value-added services in order to round out their own offerings. This was the case when Microsoft bought Skype. Another reason for buying is to reduce risk dependency in any one industry. Illinois Tool Works (ITW) is a conglomerate that buys multiple businesses in adjacent industries, such as food, hospitality, and food equipment manufacturing. That way, it is never harshly exposed to the downturns in a specific industry.

Public companies like ITW often acquire smaller companies to gain access to specific niche markets. They may also search for businesses that will provide the valuable add-on products, services, or hours to sell that are needed to meet the market's expectations of continuous quarter-over-quarter growth.

Corix, a private company, sells a wide variety of industrial equipment. It wanted to become better able to offer integrated solutions, so it bought more sophisticated vendors who could deliver engineering services that could link many products into specific environments. As a result, Corix is able to earn a higher return from integrated equipment solutions and not just lower margin stand-alone products.

Your future owner has a game plan for how he or she wants to achieve growth. Your company may be exactly what the buyer is looking for… if you do the work and make changes to your company you enable the buyer to see your business as their ideal acquisition.

When you hear the term "succession plan," you now know that it is in regards to the work you must do for two to four years before you want to sell your company. Your planning should include how you will make the business attractive to the next owner. This is the missing ingredient in succession planning advice today.

Think of the work you must do to make a business saleable as similar to the way you tailor your products and services for a specific market niche.

You don't offer your goods and services for anyone and everyone. That strategy pleases no one and has a hard time attracting fans.

Rather, the more you customize how you offer your goods and services so that you please a narrow market, the more business you do and the more new business you attract. For instance, Zappos catered to women who love to try on many pairs of shoes before settling on the perfect pair... or maybe two or three perfect pairs. Therefore, they made the shipping free and explained how easy it is to return all the shoes that didn't fit or didn't match or didn't look as good as the photo had suggested.

The strategy to make your business saleable follows the same logic: Remodel or restructure to become more aligned with what truly motivates the buyer. Thinking of it this way makes it easier for you to step into the mind of a buyer.

Up until now, your business operation has evolved to suit your style, your needs, and your financial lifestyle expectations.

For instance, if you are good at keeping the numbers in your head and like to keep some secrets away from employees about how you service your customers, then that inclination might make you disinclined to automate your procedures, keep track of what is done for customers, or mentor your staff.

When you have kept all that knowledge to yourself, then to prospective buyers, your business is not-transferrable... and not saleable. They don't know what is inside your head and can't access that knowledge unless you stay with the business. Therefore, your business has no value to them because it would take too much work to download it from you to the remaining management team.

Some owners have experience and skills that are critical to the functioning of the business. They are in rainmaker roles, or are essential to creating the next product road map or solving particularly complex problems – the services that the customers rely on.

If these functional roles cannot be taken over by key employees who have the same or a greater capability than the owner, then buyers see this as a big risk and, again, do not see a fit for their needs.

The business gave you a career, but now you have to consider how the next owner is going to get growth and continued success without you in the picture.

If you like being in control, being in the lead, and being the one who gets results, then this transition can be emotionally and psychologically challenging. Transitioning knowledge, roles, and leadership is one of the big reasons why it can take two to four years to make the business transferrable and ultimately saleable. The other big change you need to make is in how information and knowledge is captured, processed, shared, and tracked.

Building information systems will allow your company to grow – they make the business scalable, and if someone leaves, knowledge doesn't flow out the door with them. It's embedded in the company. Let's look at a case study of what can happen if you don't truly learn to embed knowledge, systems, tracking metrics, and empowerment in your staff. There were two partners in this company. One was the rainmaker. The business grew because of his skillful deal making. But the time had come to find a way to get a return on their investment in the business. The rainmaker committed to his partner that they would make the business saleable. He decided to promote the top sales person into the role of sales manager and account manager.

Then he waited to see how well the sales manager did in comparison to how well he himself did the job. You might already see the problem with this strategy. The owner did both rainmaking and sales management. The promoted sales person had no management experience and was put in a role outside his core strengths… and needed management mentoring. Of course, the new sales manager did not work in the same way the owner had. The promoted employee was on a steep learning curve to become a sales manager at the same time he was expected to continue winning work as a top sales person. This was hardly a recipe for success.

The second mistake in this example is a trap into which many leaders fall. Rather than focus on mentoring and guiding the employee in order to set him up for success, the owner would often criticize how the employee was spending his time. Tactical actions were discussed in detail while the big-picture reasons for doing something were forgotten.

When challenged, the owner said that he wanted to make sure he had made a good decision in hiring his replacement, so he was always testing him to see if he paid attention to the right things… rather than trusting he had made a good decision and supporting with acknowledgement and strategic help.

In actuality, the owner didn't want his new sales manager to be successful. He couldn't cope with the idea that someone could drive the business better than he could. So he then felt strangely satisfied to see the evidence that the promoted employee failed in his eyes. However his business partner was not impressed with how this experiment went.

Being right that there was no one who could be a rainmaker and a sales manager as well as he could was the owner's secret goal. He still needed to be the hero. He had not created an equally or more satisfying new role for himself to replace being the guy who brought in the money. Despite his promise, he did not know how to let go. This situation is typical of some of the issues owners struggle with in making a company saleable.

Making a business saleable is about making attitudinal changes in how you lead, mentor, delegate, empower, and operate your business. Part of the work of becoming transferrable and attractive to a buyer is to recognize what situations you will find hard to let go of and to replace the feeling or reward you get from such actions with roles you find equally fulfilling.

Imagine this for a minute. If you change the way you lead, promote people, install systems, and take a mentoring role in your business, then the reward could be profoundly life changing. A saleable business is like holding a winning lottery ticket in your hand. Like the advertisements say, "You have to buy a ticket to be in the running to win." Will you buy your ticket and make your business saleable?

Why is this decision so critical for your future? Take a look at the graph in Figure 3.

There are 3.6 million business owners in North America, which is represented by the dark gray bar in Figure 3. The light gray bar is the number of owners who, between 2005 and 2007, said that they wanted to sell over the next five years – 2.5 million. More than five years have passed since owners told PWC[3,4] in a study carried out by this accounting firm, that they wanted to claim their wealth. We wanted to know what really happened. So we did some digging with CapitalIQ, the people who track the sale of businesses.

---

3   McMann, Carey, SME Research LLC September 2012 http://www.exitrak.com/download.php?name=Baby_Boomer_Sell_Off.pdf

4   PriceWaterhousecoopers Business Exit Surveys http://www.pwc.com/gx/en/pwc-family-business-survey/index.jhtml

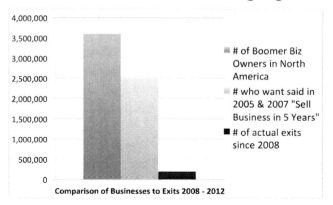

The Odds Are Challenging

Comparison of Businesses to Exits 2008 - 2012

Legend:
- # of Boomer Biz Owners in North America
- # who want said in 2005 & 2007 "Sell Business in 5 Years"
- # of actual exits since 2008

Sources: SBA, PWC, Pinnacle Equity, CFIB, Capital

Figure 3 – Understanding the Odds of a Successful Exit[5]

The tiny black bar in Figure 3 is the number of non-family exits since 2008. Shocking, isn't it?

That's right. Business owners appeared to make a decision about exiting, but few were able to do so. When the economy went into a recession, about one million business owners decided to adjust their exit dates. However, those that continued with their plan to find a buyer obviously went through a very difficult process trying to sell their businesses. Remember the misconception that many business owners have: They believe they can exit within six to twelve months should they desire. Yet, more than five years later, few had succeeded.

It's not like they didn't try. When we requested the numbers from Capital IQ, we asked them to tell us how many mid-market businesses had sold in that five-year period. Their statistics show that 199,474 exits were completed since 2008, which

---

5   Bruce, D. D. (2005). Succession Can Breed Success. Canadian Federation of Independent Business. http://www.cfib-fcei.ca/english/research/canada/224-business_ issues/251 succession_can_breed_success.html

means that as many as 1.7 million attempted to sell or exit their companies. They either failed to find buyers or didn't close the deals with willing buyers.

From our discussions with business brokers, buyers, and lenders, it is apparent that business owners arrive at their exit decisions believing they can sell the business within the year they want out. Without advice to the contrary, they proceed to attempt to sell a business that has not been made saleable. As a result, buyers have walked away because they do not see a strategic fit with their needs and goals.

Obviously, there is a failure here to communicate what buyers want and what sellers need to do to actualize their goals to sell and meet buyer needs.

Having spoken with many business owners who have attempted to sell, we found that advisors had not made them aware of what buyers look for in their acquisitions search. Owners are told to prepare succession plans, not to make their companies transferrable, growing and saleable before they contemplate contacting a broker. M&A professionals attempt to work with what an owner presents to them in order to get a deal done.

The M&A Advisor or Broker are not consultants willing to spend time making that business saleable. Owners discover their companies are un-saleable from the experience of being rejected by a succession of prospects who rifle through their due diligence packages and don't see what they are looking for. Therefore, the businesses are left on the shelf.

If you hadn't purchased this book, then you would be in the same boat as 90% of business owners across North America: unaware that your company is un-saleable and unaware of what you have to do in order to turn your company into a winning lottery ticket. You are getting this nasty piece of news now. You are paying attention. You are very likely to get that big return on your investment because you are now investing in finding out what it takes to get that big payday when you want it.

The trick to increasing the odds in your favor is to learn how to convert that ticket you already own (your business) into a winning ticket. A saleable company is in demand. An un-saleable company eventually has to close.

You are the kind of business owner who cares about the legacy you leave behind. You want to make your business saleable because it's the right thing to do for your employees, your customers, your supply chain, and your local economy; it's not just for the family bank account. You want your business to continue to succeed without you for the sake of all the stakeholders. That's a legacy of which to be very proud.

Imagine leaving your company as a legacy that rewards your community, employees, and customers. You are a leader in your economic community. What you do and how you conduct your business makes a big difference. What you do touches so many people. Making your company saleable solidifies your legacy. It lives on even if you are not at the helm anymore. It dies if your company eventually winds down and closes.

Un-saleable companies do eventually close, taking away jobs, a community's vitality, and the owner's wealth. I invite you to join us in our collective quest for a vibrant future by making your business saleable.

I want to make four distinctions about what it means to be saleable. These distinctions will help you understand why so few owners with successful businesses are making it to the finish line. These distinctions are even more critical when you think about the magnitude of the game you are about to start learning how to play.

With 2.5 million boomer businesses wanting to exit and an average of fifteen thousand known transactions per year, it is already a buyers' market. However, before you think your chances are slim and that you'll be counted as a winner only if you are lucky, let me give you another stunning number. Strategic buyers, other boomer business owners, and private equity and immigrant investors have a combined ten trillion dollars of wealth waiting to invest in companies like yours.

But they want what they want just like you would if you were to go looking for an acquisition for your company. You need to know how to rise to the top of the pack and increase the chances your company will cash-out big.

The following distinctions about being saleable will dispel some big myths. This is the bad news that is hard to grapple with.

Distinction 1 – Most Companies are Un-saleable

It is true that most companies are not saleable even if it is successful and profitable now. What this means is that another owner cannot easily step into your shoes and get the results you get.

Your company is successful for you, so why would anyone else not want it? It's almost offensive, isn't it? Stand in the shoes of a buyer. If they can't do what you do, then how can they be profitable? This is one of the reasons why we are seeing such low "selling success" rates.

This sounds like common sense, but business owners don't think this way about their companies… but they do think strategically about how to position their products and services to grow sales.

A big part of what buyers are looking for (especially if you don't want to work for the new owner) is that you have mentored and groomed talented managers who have proven they have what it takes to lead the business and achieve your growth plans.

How do you prove your team can do that? Let them take the reins two years before you plan to put the business on the market. Mentor them, and set them up for success. That may require you to learn to let go, mentor, trust and delegate.

Distinction 2 – Buyers Search for Saleable Companies

Most buyers acquire companies to satisfy goals of either a financial or a strategic nature, or both. Your company has to become what they are looking for.

This idea may sound strange and discomfiting, as if you have to completely remodel everything you've built. I'm not suggesting that.

What you may have to do to is become more focused on a narrower target market. Professionalize your operational practices so that knowledge lives in your IT system, not in people's memories, and everyone works towards goals that keep you in alignment.

Study who is buying companies in your niche and determine what they are missing that you have. Then, focus your business on growing market share and profitability in order to deliver that missing ingredient to your customers. Be brilliant at delivering your secret sauce. Your company will be noticed by your ideal buyers.

Distinction 3 – Learn to Become Saleable

There is a big difference between managing your company in its day-to-day operations and leading the change process so that it becomes saleable.

You can't expect to attract a buyer this year if you haven't done the work to make it saleable. I'm not saying you won't be able to sell it if you put it on the market now. But if your goal is to maximize your walking-away cash and increase the probability you will attract a buyer, then spend your time shaping the company to be what your ideal buyer looks for even if you aren't ready to completely walk away yet. Even if you aren't thinking of selling for another three, five, or even more years.

A saleable company gives you options. For instance, you may want to take some chips off the table by selling a minority interest in the company and participate in a bigger sale later. You may choose to step back into an advisory role or to keep running the company for the next owner and grow it together with the power of the new resources the buyer brings.

You might find that you need a General Manager to grow the business by fifteen or twenty percent if that is not your expertise. That General Manager might become your ideal buyer after reaching the agreed upon performance targets. Alternatively, he or she may just run the business for you while you go on to your next act until the right buyer emerges.

You may want to explore selling to all your employees by learning more about ESOPs, Employee Stock Ownership Plans, which, when executed professionally, can also get you to an exit over a period of years.

With all the options available to you as the owner of a saleable company, you may also choose to sell, walk away completely, and move on to your next act.

Any of these options are possible when you make a company saleable.

It's a beautiful thing to witness an owner make this transformation from frustrated yet successful to unburdened and delighted, with a more profitable and saleable asset. This commitment to becoming saleable gives you short-term profitability and a long-term, wealth-building winning ticket.

Distinction 4 – Use Advisors

Making an exit is complicated. When you want to exit may not align with when buyers are looking. Selecting your ideal buyer may require substantial changes within your organization. Leading strategy and change may not be your strength. A consultant would help you prepare and lead the changes with you.

If you want your family members to become the buyers, there is a lot of preparatory work that needs to be done to help them get there. First and foremost is that this has to be their idea – not yours. They may need several years to be ready to lead the business, or they may tell you this is not what they envision for their future. Family dynamics and ingrained communication blocks may require a family coach.

Many owners have potential tax consequences they didn't know about and such problems need to be resolved years before an exit takes place. Sitting down with a tax specialist once you know the type of buyer you are aiming for will help you clean up any brewing problems.

Making all these changes can bring up all kinds of resistance in you like it did in the owner who wasn't able to let go of his identity as a rainmaker to help make his employee successful. Behaviors like these are hard to spot. A good coach can help you get out of your own way and build a transition plan so that you can get your needs met and make the changes needed.

Your relationship with your bank might need to change. Perhaps you need growth capital or management buyout financing. Letting your banker in on your plans enables them to help prepare you and your company to be in a position to borrow funds. Also, buyers won't make decisions about moving forward with an offer without getting insight into how your company makes money, spends money, and tracks money.

Your accountant will be needed to help you clean up your books. A financial analyst can refine your reporting and tracking systems so that you can find profitability leaks sooner and fix them before the bottom-line result at year end makes your stomach churn.

If your next act in life requires a certain level of cash flow and your family commitments or needs for retirement are unknown, you will want to work with a financial and wealth planner to get a reality check on what you have and what you really need.

These steps need to be fully planned out before you start on this journey. To make your company saleable, you must leave behind your operator days with your great-lifestyle paycheck and your operator ways of thinking, planning, and acting. You adopt the mindset of the company's primary investor and build your asset's value. Creating a blueprint for each of the steps is essential to getting you where you want to go.

Chapter 2 Summary

What to take away from this chapter:

- Why most companies are un-saleable.

- What buyers are looking for.

- How a saleable company widens your options for how you and your business can split up, reward everyone, and give you and your family a secure next act.

- That making a business saleable and then planning your exit is complicated and that it's important to use advisors that are knowledgeable about selling a business to help you get to your goal and destination.

- Shifting your mindset to lead the changes to make your company saleable can be an emotionally charged experience where old habits are hard to break.

A custom Saleability Blueprint keeps you on track and making the right changes in your business so that your ideal buyers are ready to put an offer on the table for an amount that could be substantially more than what your company is worth today.

CHAPTER 3

CRACKING THE DEALMAKERS' CODE

This is what you will learn in this chapter:

- How we uncovered buyers' and lenders' secrets.

- How buyers think about their acquisition goals and their reasoning for thinking that way.

- Why so many companies are un-saleable from the buyer's perspective.

So, you might be asking, "What is a Saleability Blueprint?" and "Will making my business saleable work for my business?"

Let's tackle the first question. In a nutshell, a Saleability Blueprint is a customized list of the things that need to be changed in your business and in how you lead it in order to make your business saleable.

The blueprint is built following our proven four-step system. Each step has many questions to ponder. We will discuss these steps individually later, and you will look at the issues that are important to you and compare them to the reality of your personal and business situations. Some avenues for moving forward will naturally fall away as you work through the questions, and other options that you had not considered may become the correct path for you. The answers to these questions point you in a particular direction and form your Saleability Blueprint.

Now, let's consider the second question, "Will making my business saleable work for my business?" Without being able to specifically address the unique aspects of each business owner, let's go over a list of situations where making even some changes in the business won't make it any more saleable than it is today.

- DECLINING FORTUNES The company used to be successful but has been in decline for several years. Without repurposing the products or services or reinventing how it does business, it is difficult to come back from this situation. Buyers are acquiring the future. Some buyers will acquire turnaround situations, but be prepared for selling at a bargain-basement number. In some cases, the company has to be right-sized to deal with the new economic environment, such as any company that makes materials for the home-building industry or forestry industry.

- OWNER OPERATED Many businesses are run by the owner. The distinction here is that the employees are all tactical and the owner is responsible for all strategy, sales, and product development and for running the business. When you do it all, there is nothing to sell.

- PROJECT-BASED BUSINESSES There are hugely successful companies that sell their services in the form of projects, such as construction, HVAC, and professional services like medical, legal and financial. These companies are saleable when there is predictability and consistency with how the company finds and wins the project work and when they are counterbalanced with more reliable revenues from services or product sales.

- SUNSET INDUSTRIES We've all seen the effect of the pace of change on once-industry-leading champions, such as Research in Motion; Kodak; businesses that provided services for typewriters, fax machines, and book retailers; and any business that doesn't keep up with the pace of rapid change (the music industry).

So, how did we learn about what types of companies can be made saleable and then develop our four-step system to help businesses transform into what buyers search for?

My husband, Rob, and I are management consultants, not business brokers. We designed our system so it works with all the types of companies that we have had the privilege of working with. We wrote the book Fast-Track Secrets for Making Your Business Saleable based on our success with helping our clients work through our four-step saleability system. We guide them through the plan and then get in there and help them implement it.

In short, we've helped many entrepreneurs uncover how to get their valuation growth and their walk-away cash.

I've also been in mergers and acquisitions since 2002 as a member of the Association of Corporate Growth (ACG), which is comprised of intermediaries that facilitate deal making between buyers and sellers for mid-market firms, those companies with ten million to one hundred million dollars in revenue who are the backbone of our economy – businesses owned by people like you.

I was invited to join the board of the ACG Vancouver Chapter and eventually became president in 2008. ACG monitors the deal making community, and their latest survey validates what most advisors are already noticing: More owners are putting their companies on the market. And, the latest statistics from ACG and Merrill DataSite show that forty-three percent of buyers intend to be more active in buying companies than they have been since the 2008 financial crisis.

Furthermore, when added together, private equity, strategic buyers, family businesses, immigrant investors, and new entrepreneurs have that combined ten trillion dollars in wealth sitting on the side lines waiting to be invested in current, established businesses like yours.

It is good to begin to prepare for that big exit in the next few years. The longer owners wait, the more it becomes a buyers' market, and at that 10% success rate, the odds are already stacked high.

For just over a decade, I've met the Dealmakers, the people who buy and transact the sales of businesses. Meeting a business owner (or people like us) is rare in these circles. Dealmakers speak a very different language from that of business owners and management consultants. It is a hard code to crack. You don't need to invest your time in trying to figure them out. You just need the formula to make your company into what they look for and let the experts make the connection for you.

Over the years of working with Dealmakers, I saw a huge problem. Problems to me are gold. They are opportunities to fill a need. This is what I witnessed:

- Buyers never talk to business owners until they are sitting across the table from them after the owner has put the company on the market.

- Business owners never talk to intermediaries (the brokers and M&A advisors) until they want to sell.

You see, there is a big divide between these worlds. They don't talk to you, and you don't talk to them.

What really struck home was the magnitude of this problem. I found out that the typical buyer looks at as many as five hundred to nine hundred deals each year. Then, they buy only two to five companies. Throughout our discourse, those buyers shared with me the list of reasons why they don't buy.

After a bit of further digging, I got them to reveal to me what they wish business owners would do long before they try to sell. In short, they gave me the formula that allowed me to crack their code, and that code is what we use to guide all our clients. It's what I want to show to you.

Dealmakers have money to burn. The trillions have been piling up since 2008 – in private equity funds, on the balance sheets of big corporations who need to make acquisitions to get growth, from private individuals who want to buy a growing company, and from mid-sized companies who want to add to their platform offerings.

Dealmakers want deals and expect to close a lot of them, but they can't find what they are looking for.

This is where you come in.

By making your business saleable, your business becomes exactly what buyers want… and it gets you your winning lottery ticket. A saleable company is:

- A great deal for a Dealmaker.

- A great deal for the lender financing the buyout of your business.

- Bright futures for your employees who have helped

you get to this pivotal point in your financial life.

- A relief to your suppliers and vendors who rely on your business to keep their businesses humming.

- A great deal for you and your family.

Unfortunately for both Dealmakers and business owners, that persistent rumor that you can sell just by calling a broker is preventing the message from getting through to business owners that they need to remodel their companies to be what buyers want.

So, why do we have this sorry state of affairs?

Dealmakers aren't out on the road educating sellers on how to become attractive enough to be bought. They don't have to because brokers are lined up at their door showing them companies they might be interested in buying.

You would think that your key business advisors like your accountant, lawyer, insurance agent, consultant, coach, financial planner, banker, or wealth advisor would have alerted you that there was more to an exit than making the decision to sell and then calling an M&A professional.

However, the buying and selling of companies is a specialty area of expertise. Advisors often don't learn about each other's specialties except anecdotally. Every advisor knows an owner needs a strategy for succession to enable an exit. But not how to prepare so an exit is possible.

Advisors do work with Dealmakers, but they don't have occasion to understand the deeper detail of their arcane practices. Buyers don't tend to reveal their strategies and playbooks to outsiders. It's a complicated world. So, what stories are shared tend to underplay what actually goes on behind closed doors.

The field of exit planning is in its infancy. An exit planner helps an owner through all the steps so they are ready to do a deal. But is an exit plan all you need? No. You need to build value and transferability.

What we do and what our Saleability Blueprint enables you to do is ensure that true value is built inside the company. Buyers and lenders need to see possibility, and nothing predicts possibility and potential better than a history of steady, consistent growth in either accelerating or stable industries.

That's what we do. Let's be honest; before you read this book, did you believe you would have no problem selling your business one day?

Despite the fact that your advisors have not suggested that becoming saleable is imperative to enable claiming the wealth you have built up inside your business, hopefully, you are gaining confidence. Trust that making your business saleable is the right solution for you and your family's financial future. If it is your dream to be able to find a buyer for your business and ensure continuity after you leave, then learning about this four-step process is your next step.

Recognizing the predicament caused by the great disconnect between business owners and Dealmakers was a big lightbulb moment for me. Here was a huge problem staring me in the face, and I, being a management consultant, could see it from both sides of the deal – the owner's perspective and the buyer's perspective. The big problem all boils down to lack of critical information exchange and guidance at the right time and from the right source.

To help you understand the disconnect between you, the business owner, and the sea of buyers who might well want to acquire a business like yours if certain aspects of the operation were changed, fixed, or added, here are more critical distinctions:

Distinction 1 – Starting Too Late

A business owner doesn't normally get to meet buyers and see their acquisition criteria until they want to sell. By that time, it's too late to do anything to become what buyers are looking for. Unless the owner learns what the buyer is looking for two to four years before the desired exit date and makes those changes, the owner may never get close to meeting their ideal buyer, never mind being able to receive an offer. Buyers become superb pattern recognizers since they spend so much time shopping for right-fit businesses. All they need to do is scan the offering package your M&A professional sends out to know if they even want to talk further. The buyers' minds are made up; they want to acquire what they are looking for. Unless the owner has absolutely everything in place in preparation for this encounter, a deal won't even get out of the starting gate and the more prepared competitors' businesses will be purchased.

Distinction 2 – Access to Buyers' Criteria

Business owners to date have had no access to the acquisition criteria.

That acquisition criteria is a black box, a deep mystery. This really is the heart of the matter. If you had access to that information years before you wanted to exit, then you would know exactly what you had to do to sell your company. Furthermore, you would dramatically increase the probability that you would be able to sell and for possibly millions more than it is worth today.

Access to that inside information is now in your hands

Our four-step system asks you the questions that point out which issues may be a problem for you because they are part of the buyer's black box. You can get that information now, when you need it, so that you can change the course of your future.

Distinction 3 – Skipping Steps and Missing the Right Steps

A business that has been made saleable so that it is attractive to the next owner is often more profitable for the current owner. The questions we ask in the four-step system point you to discover typical profitability challenges that we call "buyer red flags," which you will learn more about in the next chapter.

When you have more consistent profitability, you have more options for finding the buyer that best suits your interests, business type, and future. If that weren't enough in itself, there are more benefits...

- Imagine having no more doubts about selling/not selling. You have set a date to claim your wealth, and you are doing something to make sure you get there.

- Imagine seeing this year's financial statements with a much improved profitability number. You have more cash to make changes and to give your company the resources it needs.

- Imagine building a powerful future that you look forward to, one in which you're living the life you want and doing the very things that make you feel vibrant and alive, things that make a difference.

- Imagine no more worries about what will happen to your employees, suppliers, and customers. You are leaving a legacy that takes care of everyone's needs.

This is what we mean by having a powerful, desired end result. You set your intention and your focus so you get what you really want.

My absolute best advice to you is this: Keep reading so you get to know the acquisition criteria and how buyers think of value. Then, you can make those changes that put thousands or millions more in your wealth management account and increase the likelihood that you will be able to sell your company and win your financial, professional, and personal freedom. It's how you will leave a sound legacy for your business family.

To take advantage of these strategies, you have to let go of that wealth-destroying idea that you will be able to sell your company whenever you want and all you need is someone to take over your job.

How do we know that so many business owners believe that they can wait to plan their exit whenever they finally feel like selling the business?

We regularly speak with bankers, wealth managers, M&A professionals, business brokers, and lawyers. They have file cabinets full of stories about owners who got caught having to sell because of unforeseen circumstances right when their businesses were having a difficult year.

Every advisor attempts to speak with their clients about their exit plans. Most owners have been pitched numerous times by investment banks promising to be able to sell the business if they just come to a seminar. Owners have become wary to such pressure.

Therefore, the exit question brings up irritable reactions that are hard to break through; so, the topic is dropped.

As we work directly with business owners, we know that beneath the irritation is a dog's breakfast of confusion, misinformation, fear, anxiety, and Catch-22 situations.

Do you shove away this most important financial strategy because of any of these reasons?

- ❑ I'll exit when I'm good and ready.

- ❑ I'd be a sell out if I sold.

- ❑ My child is a bit young to take over the business.

- ❑ My partner doesn't want to talk about it.

- ❑ My wife is always bugging me to retire. What would I do then?

- ❑ I like what I do; why would I sell it?

- ❑ Who would I become if I didn't have this work to keep me occupied?

- ❑ I'm not going to let my competitor see my books.

- ❑ I don't see how this whole thing is going to work. It's too risky. I've got a good income now; why would I jeopardize that?

- ❑ I'm not old enough to sell the business.

- ❑ I've got too much on my plate right now to deal with an exit that is still years away.

- ❑ I'll just keep pulling money out of the business. That will keep us financially afloat.

- ❑ What about my employees? What would happen to them if I sold to someone who then fired them? I couldn't live with myself.

- ❏ I've got enough put away. I don't need to get greedy.

- ❏ I don't want to deal with a snake-oil salesman to get my business sold.

- ❏ If I sell, then that means that I've come to the end of my useful life. I'm not ready for feeling like that.

- ❏ If I sell I have to give up my monthly salary and dividends for a one-time payout. That's it, no more gravy train. Why would I do that?

- ❏ I've heard I've got to really cut back costs two years before I sell, including salaries. I don't see how we can run the business that way.

- ❏ Making it saleable means costly advisors. I can't afford all that overhead.

Every one of these worries has a solution to it. It's called making a new choice based on what is important to you. Keep reading and you will uncover for yourself the reasons that make it a good decision for you to either maintain your company the way it is, or choose the wealth generating path by making it saleable.

If you need a reminder about the merits of making better choices for yourself, your family, and your business, because these concerns are gnawing away at the back of your mind, then just remember the statistics we quoted from our research with Capital IQ and other sources:

- • There are 3.6 million business owners.

- • 70% wanted to sell in the last five years.

- • 199,474 actually got the deal done.

- • 1.7 million owners who wanted to sell are still running their un-saleable companies today or have closed. These business owners are unaware of how to position their company so that they maximize the return on their investments.

- There is $10 trillion in wealth looking for saleable businesses.

Chapter 3 Summary

Here are the takeaways from this chapter:

- Choose how you will exit ahead of time so you have plenty of time to make the changes that make your business saleable.

- Buyers acquire the companies that best fit their strategic focus. Uncover what that is well in advance and align your business accordingly.

- Selecting your ideal acquirer involves asking and answering numerous questions that help you pinpoint a strategy that meets all your needs and is in the best interests of your company and its stakeholders.

- You will need to follow the proven four-step framework to create a custom Saleability Blueprint to fit your needs, aspirations and business challenges. Following the Blueprint reduces the confusion and complexity inherent in leading change.

CHAPTER 4

THE FOUR STEP FRAMEWORK TO BECOME SALEABLE

This is what you will learn about in this chapter:

- The personal and professional questions you will answer as you move through the four-step framework to become saleable.

- Step 1 of the four-step saleability system.

The four steps to becoming Saleable are sequential. The questions themselves, as well as assistance with developing your answers, can be found in the *Fast-Track Secrets for Making Your Business Saleable* book and playbook. This chapter gives you an introduction and overview of the work involved so that you can better decide if you are ready to embark on this journey.

The finished product you will have after reading this book and working through the questions in the *Fast-Track Secrets for Making Your Business Saleable Playbook* is what we call your "Saleability Blueprint."

The answers to these questions help shape your plan that will help you:

- Handle Reality

- Hone Goals and Decisions

- Hunt the Right Acquirer

- Helm the Transition

Step 1 – Handle Reality

Your first step is not about the business.

It's about you. What is important to you? Consider your family and the people your business touches. Tackling questions in this area will help you unlock your interests so that you are thinking about what you do want, not what you don't want. You may encounter emotionally difficult issues that require further exploration or an uncomfortable trade-off. That's okay. You have to know your full reality in order to shape it into the future reality you desire.

Getting ready to transition from full-time business owner to an owner that is preparing to move away from the helm can be a highly charged time in your life. Facing your emotions helps you let go and take charge… something that unprepared business owners do not do and then, accordingly, they can't take that final step to sell.

A father and son in a construction-related industry fell into this emotional trap. The father had built a successful business. He invited his son, who had strong business acumen, in to help him build it up to the next level. The son weighed the invitation and asked his father what his intentions were, long-term, with the business.

The father confirmed they would build it together and then sell it. The son joined the business, and they succeeded. Within a few years, the son could see it was the right time to start preparing the company for sale. He made the suggestion to his father, reminding him of their agreement, and described his rationale for why this was the ideal time to attract a buyer – they had consistent profitability and their industry was consolidating.

The father said he would think about it. The son kept bringing it up and asked for a date when the decision would be made. Time passed. He beseeched his father, describing what would happen if they couldn't sell. Their family wealth might be depleted if the business couldn't grow further. In fact, without further capital injection, the company would find it hard to position itself as a bigger player in the industry against the newly consolidated bigger companies.

The father finally told his son he didn't want to sell. He could not see what he would do if he was not the president of a multimillion dollar company. He was paralyzed with the fear that selling meant his life was over.

While the son had compassion for his father, he kept pushing for his father to change his mind. One day, push came to shove and the father fired his son. He also injected all his fear and frustration into his parting message. "I will prove you wrong. I will continue to build this firm without you and show you how it's done. You don't believe I can do it!"

The son was devastated. The father and son did not talk again. All the son could do was watch as what he had predicted came to be in a short three years.

The industry did change because of consolidation, creating a far bigger competitive environment for the company. His father was unable to retain some key clients without his son's expertise beside him. Soon, other valuable employees started to leave.

Today, this company is a shell of its former self. The father, now in his late sixties, has to keep working. There is no nest egg on which his family can retire. Sadly, the son and the father still do not talk.

In Step 1 – Handle Reality, you will discover what emotional ties sit unexamined in your life so that they don't surprise you when you most need to take action. Awareness and ability to recognize your own strong emotions is a part of growing a business. They inform you about what's important to you and give you information about what needs to change. Ignore them at your peril.

You won't be able to make the changes inside your company to become saleable until you've uncovered those emotional ties and barriers that bind you to your employees, your legacy, and your identity.

If you wait to deal with your emotions until you suddenly find yourself staring at the line awaiting your signature to close the deal, then you will find yourself like so many other business owners – unable to take this last step.

How big is this problem?

Our research with brokers and buyers reveals a sad story. The number one reason why a company doesn't sell is that the owner did not make the company saleable. Reason number two is that owners have not done their emotional preparation. They are unable to let go.

It's time for you to start letting go of your role, of your identity as the owner. Let go of your interest in having the company work to suit your needs rather than satisfying the next owner's requirements to say yes to acquiring your business.

If you don't let go now, then when a potential buyer comes to call, you won't be ready. Interested buyers search for their acquisitions when they need a business like yours to power their growth… not when you are necessarily ready to sell. You want your business to be saleable as soon as possible so that you can meet luck with preparation. You might not realize it, but buyers constantly scour the marketplace, looking for bright, beautiful, and bold businesses to buy. Yours will be spotted if you are having an impact in your niche.

Furthermore, if you don't let go now and try to sell later, then when you have to sell and haven't done both the emotional and business preparation, you will then have to deal with the devastating feeling of disappointment like the father and son with the construction business did. Today, the father is estranged from his family and struggling to make ends meet. He cannot provide for his family by claiming his wealth in a business sale as he had promised, and he is tormented with regret, shame, and resentment.

Is he alone in this dilemma? No. As the statistics show, there were 2.5 million business owners who said they would sell within five years. Only 1.7 million attempted it, and of those, only 199,474 succeeded.

Will you be facing disappointment rather than a future you really want? If you work to make your company saleable, then you won't have to face…

…Disappointment that you did not learn it was important to you to be able to claim the wealth tied up in your business.

…Disappointment that you did not take the steps to understand what was important to you and your family before it was too late to undo the damage.

…Disappointment that you missed the window of opportunity in which you could sell your company to a buyer that would take it to the next level of growth.

...Disappointment in yourself that you didn't unlock and deal with the issues that kept you tied to your company.

...Or disappointment that the market has changed and your business isn't riding the crest of the growth wave any longer; it's on the decline... a melting asset that is hard to manage, never mind sell.

Clearly, it's not business savvy or good for the heart to set yourself up for disappointment. So, again, it's time to start letting go of your role, your identity as the owner, and your interest in having the company work to suit your needs.

1. To be saleable, you can't be in a functional role on which the business depends.

2. To be saleable, you have to be psychologically ready to move on with enthusiasm rather than looking back as if your best days are behind you.

3. To be saleable, your company has to become what the next owner needs it to be.

The Fork in the Road – a Decision Point

We call this step coming to terms with what's true about your business. You have come to a fork in the road. To capture the value of all you have built and solidify your gains, you have to decide well in advance that you and your business will be separating. It needs to continue to thrive and grow so that all stakeholders get their needs met. As for you, life will never be empty and meaningless after your exit because you are moving on to a new act that you look forward to.

Some owners never recognize that there is a choice to be made at the fork in the road. They continue to work inside their business and not on the strategic direction of the company.

While employees and family may see the owner's lack of energy, focus, and attention to company direction, the owner may not. I have noticed that single-owner companies often don't have trusted advisors who can give them clear feedback about their situations. Partnerships and multiple-owner businesses do often see one another aging and slowing down and are used to offering observations that result in new decisions being made.

In the Handle Reality step, you will want to find people who can effectively break through to you with timely heads-up messages.

Every company goes through the stages of start up, build, breakthrough, growth, and stability. Every owner goes up the same learning curve: you start your business; learn how to build it; and ride the adventure to grow it. Then comes the time you realize you have a valuable asset that needs to be liquidated in order to claim the value that has been built. Yet, if you miss that fork in the road, then you also miss out on the prime time to sell a company that still has growth potential.

At that inflection point, where growth needs more capital and the owner needs more leadership leverage, is the time to make the choice.

Regardless of whom the buyer is, from family members to a professional buyer, each buyer type will have to deal with these requirements for capital infusion and the need for more sophisticated leadership and management.

Your Business Journey

Figure 4 – Your Journey versus Your Company's Journey

Every owner goes through the same stages in their business life. Transitioning ownership is how you keep developing the company's value so that it rewards all the stakeholders in your world – from your family to your employees.

You have come to that time when your paths are moving in different directions.

To get the return you want, it's time to let the business go to the next level with a new owner and for you to cash in on your hard work.

Accepting these facts helps you handle reality.

So, your first step in handling reality is to recognize your own value and your own accomplishments. Look at your company and see everything that you've built. When you take this vital step, you don't need to wait for other people to demonstrate to you that what you have built is worth something. You have to value it yourself instead of looking for others to value it whether by praise and adulation or with an inflated, unsubstantiated offer.

You have to understand the difference between what you value and how a buyer would value your company. These two ideas are very different. You must let go of the idea that your company's valuation is tied to the success of all you have built in your life and in your company. So, by your valuing all you have done, you can let go of the need to have a prospective buyer "demonstrate to you" that your company has value during your negotiation.

If you are in the room negotiating with a willing buyer, recognize you've already been vetted as valuable and leave the need to prove anything in the hallway. This is the ultimate step in letting go: refusing to let the value determined by a third party mean something about the value of all you have accomplished. Own your own value as a business owner. Separate it from the value of your business now, and move on to the next step.

You have every right to be proud. You have built a remarkable company and worked hard to move past every obstacle. Look at the lives you've touched. Your employees are able to have careers and support their families because of you. You've solved problems and served your customers. Your suppliers have also built great businesses because of your success. Own your accomplishments.

Now, take your next step in handling reality. Change your perspective! Realize that the way you are going to become saleable is to see the company through the buyer's eyes, not your eyes. Don't expect the buyer and lender to acknowledge all you have gone through to get where you are. That's your job.

Now imagine stepping back from the picture.

You take more of a strategic role and are no longer involved in the day-to-day operations of the company. Your role is now about maximizing your sale value, and to do that, you must get the business ready for the next owner. You are confident in the team you have put in place, and everything is humming along nicely. They are building sale value for you, hand over fist, and creating a better proposition for your buyer. You could walk away any day you choose and enjoy a huge payoff from a top quality buyer.

How does that feel?

The process of letting go happens gradually as you begin to build the vision of yourself in your next act, the next stage of your life where you are a former business owner delighting in reinventing yourself, your life, and your contributions to the world.

You are finding a new way to make a difference, and it is very fulfilling, satisfying, and such a treat to be out from under all the stress of operating your company.

Start practicing seeing yourself enjoying your life in your next act. Feel the sense of satisfaction it brings, having guided yourself to this moment of freedom and choice.

Envision your future without your business. What will form your identity? There are so many ways to leave your stamp, your legacy in this world. Your business is just one of many. Boomers today are changing the world by staying engaged and getting involved. Where will you play next?

What is Your Company Worth Today?

The next part of handling reality is to come to terms with how much your company is worth today.

You are about to learn what we call a "back of the napkin valuation calculation." An unofficial way to find out what your company is worth, it is also an easy rule of thumb that helps you set up a baseline and face reality. So, it's for your use only. I don't suggest repeating the number to anyone.

It's very important for you to understand that although your company has a certain value, it is most likely un-saleable, meaning that you would not find a buyer willing to pay you this amount.

The number you are about to discover may also disappoint you. It might not be reflective of the value that you think it should have.

Handling reality means getting comfortable with the facts: Your business is most likely un-saleable in its current state, and it's not worth what you wish it was worth. When you face these facts, then you can use the emotion of your reaction to spur you on to make it worth what you really want to sell it for. Bottle that feeling. You will need it for motivation.

Two words of caution here:

1.	This is not a number you are going to rely on to take to the bank. If the bank needs to know what your company is worth, they will use a certified business valuation expert, who takes many issues into consideration. We use the "back of the napkin" version to give you a ball-park value and to teach you the basic steps of how a company is valued.

2.	This is not a number to get attached to – or to get upset about. It is an exercise in handling reality. This number is a baseline. You are aiming for more by making your company saleable.

To start this informal, unofficial, rule of thumb, "back of the napkin" exercise, you will need to look at your income statement for last year. Find the number referred to as EBITDA, or Earnings Before Interest, Taxes, Depreciation, and Amortization, near the bottom of your income statement.

If it is a negative number, then, for the sake of the exercise, take the last year your company was profitable and use that number. This is another reason you need two to four years to make your company saleable. To be saleable, you need to show consistent, growing profit over at least a two year period, for the buyer's sake and your own.

If a professional, certified valuation expert were analyzing your financial statements, they would invariably add and detract values that would change your EBITDA number. This process is called normalization. The rationale behind this strategy is to portray the value of the business without items that would not normally be a part of the company if you weren't the owner anymore.

However, for our purposes, we will deal with the EBITDA value as it was at the end of your last fiscal year or the last year in which the business was profitable within the last three years. Next, in our preparation to help you understand what your company is valued at today, we need to investigate how the Multiple works.

The "Multiple" is a term used by the financial industry to calculate an offer. There can be a lot of confusion about what the Multiple is and what it means to you, the seller. In a professional valuation, the expert may use a variety of methods to calculate company value. We are selecting the Multiple as our tool for the "back of the napkin" valuation since it is the easiest to understand and work with.

The Multiple number is what your EBITDA will be multiplied

by to determine a potential valuation price. It is a number that you have power over if you have made your business saleable. The EBITDA number reflects the facts of your business history. The Multiple of your EBITDA is the negotiated part of the price, but it also has roots in facts. Let's understand what drives those facts.

The Multiple selected to determine valuation is driven by several factors. From the buyer perspective, they are willing to offer a Multiple that realistically defines how much cash flow will accrue from the business over the next few years. It is also narrowed down by the number of businesses in that industry sector that have sold for comparable Multiples.

For instance, technology companies often receive offers with Multiples of EBITDA of more than eight or even as high as fifteen times EBITDA. The Multiple for a professional services company, which falls into the Industrials classification, does not get anywhere near that Multiple because its cash flows don't have the same heady growth rate. Typical comparable companies within the Industrials classification are currently getting Multiples between five and eight times EBITDA or less outside of the US.

Let's look at Figure 5 so you can select which industry classification your business fits into. The chart shows you two types of buyers: strategic and financial. Strategic refers to one company acquiring another company. Financial refers to professional buying groups, otherwise known as private equity, who raise funds to invest in minority or full equity ownership of private companies like yours.

As you can see, strategic buyers make roughly 90% of all acquisitions. To the right, the Average EBITDA Multiples shows the Multiple paid to business owners in these industrial classifications. These Multiples of EBITDA change each year as more deals are done. You can see that the trend in some industries is steadily upward and that others have fallen off. The past does not predict the future across all types of business acquisitions.

Capital IQ JULY 2013 Analysis of Mergers and Acquisitions For companies LESS THAN $500 M in value											
	STRATEGIC BUYERS			FINANCIAL BUYERS			AVERAGE EBITDA				
	# of deals			# of deals			MULTIPLES				
SECTOR	2010	2011	2012	2010	2011	2012	2010	2011	2012	2013	
Consumer discretionary	1,542	2,279	2,305	302	313	357	11.2X	11.0X	10.2X	9.4X	
Consumer Staples	282	435	464	47	58	100	12.6X	7.8X	7.5X	10.1X	
Energy	928	1,117	998	27	52	107	8.7X	10.2X	6.7X	5.3X	
Healthcare	892	1,352	1,263	66	118	737	11.1X	11.7X	11.0X	10.4X	
Industrials	1,481	2,181	2,243	162	200	379	5.4X	8.3X	8.0X	6.8X	
Information Technology	1,602	2,202	2,131	113	158	938	11.1X	12.8X	8.9X	11.6X	
Materials	1,065	1,314	1,111	58	94	152	9.4X	6.8X	8.5X	6.2X	
Telecommunications Services	101	130	96	4	12	32	4.2X	5.7X	10.9X	10.9X	
Utilities	186	222	206	6	13	68	9.5X	10.3X	8.4X	28X	
TOTAL DEALS DONE	12,447	15,374	15,758	3,090	1,040	3,311					

Figure 5 – EBITDA Multiples Paid for Mid-Market Businesses 2010- 2013[6]

Like the real estate industry, in which a realtor will price your house based upon the prices of similar houses in the same neighborhood, the financial industry keeps track of the Multiples paid for businesses that sell.

From your perspective as the seller, you need to know how you can increase the Multiple applied to your business, within the range of comparable companies that have sold in your industry, by adding value to your business.

In Figure 6 are examples of specific actions that a buyer would value if they were incorporated into your business. Buyers all have their own specific acquisition criteria and will weight some

6   July 2013 S&P Capital IQ Market Observations http://img.en25.com/Web/StandardandPoors/MMO_July2013_5260.pdf

of these features more heavily than others. Having said that, each of these elements will add value to your business regardless of which buyer might find your company an attractive fit for their acquisition goals.

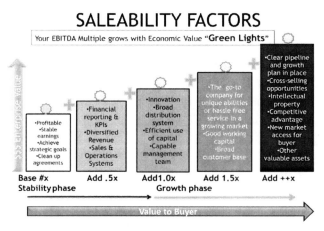

SALEABILITY FACTORS
Your EBITDA Multiple grows with Economic Value **"Green Lights"**

Base #x Stability phase	Add .5x	Add 1.0x	Add 1.5x	Add ++x
•Profitable •Stable earnings •Achieve strategic goals •Clean up agreements	•Financial reporting & KPIs •Diversified Revenue •Sales & Operations Systems	•Innovation •Broad distribution system •Efficient use of capital •Capable management team	•The go-to company for unique abilities or hassle free service in a growing market •Good working capital •Broad customer base	•Clear pipeline and growth plan in place •Cross-selling opportunities •Intellectual property •Competitive advantage •New market access for buyer •Other valuable assets

Growth phase

Value to Buyer

EBITDA: Earnings Before Interest Taxes Depreciation and Amortization

Figure 6 – Understanding the Multiple Effect

Each element described in the Multiple Effect adds what we call "saleability factors." These are the "green lights" that tell a buyer your business is worth examining to see if they want to make an offer. Buyers are also looking for red flags that tell them this company is too risky to purchase. The Multiple of EBITDA they are willing to offer goes up with the right green lights and down with every red flag they encounter as they do their due diligence… within the range of the Multiples of comparable businesses that did sell in your industry. This is how the buyer arrives at the number they are willing to offer. The higher the number of green lights your company has, then the higher the Multiple will be.

Now you have a better understanding of the factors that determine the negotiated number that will be applied to your EBIT-DA, the Multiple. Let's review before we run the numbers to see what your company is worth:

1. Find your EBITDA of your last profitable year within the last three years.

2. Select the industrial classification that your business falls into. If you need help to make that determination, then go to this website and please confer with Standard and Poors Global Industry Classification Standard (GICS)™ http://www.msci.com/resources/pdfs/MK-GICS-DIR-3-02.pdf

3. Recognize that the range of Multiples defined in your industrial classification were for businesses that have been made saleable. To undertake a "back of the napkin" calculation, we have to select a Multiple that does not reflect the green lights you have yet to add and that does reflect all the red flags that lurk in the majority of businesses, making them un-saleable. Therefore, for all companies, we use a baseline Multiple of 3 times EBITDA.

4. Setting the Multiple at 3 shows you the potential you have to grow the value of the business. It is a superb reality check and is an important part of handling reality.

Understanding your baseline is critical to learning how to close your opportunity gap: the amount you want to add to your baseline to make it worth what you want to sell your company for.

Now multiply your EBITDA by the Multiple of 3. The result is your current "back of the napkin" valuation. Think of this result as part of a range of numbers rather than a number to hang your hat on.

Your company may have some of the green lights described in Figure 6. You might have had many one-time costs in the year you selected. Put these distractions aside.

The number you have calculated is where you are starting from on your journey to become saleable, not a number to argue with or depend on for other purposes.

If a buyer (or a lender backing a potential buyer) came along today and looked at your business, then through their due diligence, they would see red flags that, today, you can't see, and they would not see all the green lights that tell them this is a company that will help them realize their growth goals. Learning to see your business through this filter helps you stand in the shoes of your ideal buyer and, even more importantly, makes you better able to psychologically let go of assigning a number based solely on what you value in your business.

Now, this very well may be a moment when hearts race, stomachs churn, and brain fog descends if the number you are staring at does not reflect the secret number you were hanging onto in your head. Yes, this is what we mean by handling reality.

If you want to be able to sell your company and do so for thousands or millions more than the number on the napkin, then follow along as we go through the next step and continue to check in with yourself.

This is the next crucial step in handling reality. You want to be honest with yourself here. Make note of the response that best reflects your current state of mind and heart, having discovered the current "back of the napkin" value of your company:

- ❑ It's higher.

- ❑ About what I thought it would be.

❑   It's lower, but I feel okay about it.

❑   It's much lower, and I don't feel good about it.

❑   I'm in shock.

If you're not feeling good about the number you are staring at, then this is not the time to try to prove that the number or the calculation is wrong. That will be a waste of your time and resources. Use this event as a signal that there is more to learn. There are changes you can make inside your company to improve the valuation number. I'll be showing you what kinds of changes shortly.

So, fortunately, there is a lot you can do to improve that valuation. Making the company saleable makes it more profitable because you build a Saleability Blueprint and learn where to place your focus in order to implement your plans for each step.

Chapter 4 Summary

What to take away from Chapter 4:

- The first step in the four-step system to make your business saleable is to handle your reality.

    o   You are not your company.

- Understand why handling reality is a crucial first step and the key to unlocking the future you really want.

    o   You can have a life after you sell.

- How a buyer assesses the value of your business and why it might not reflect the same opinion of value that you have.

- How to determine what your company is worth today.

  ○ Your company is an asset that you own.

- How to come to terms with your business' current value versus what you would like to sell it for.

  ○ You have an opportunity to increase the value.

CHAPTER 5

GET TO KNOW YOUR DESIRED END RESULT

What you will learn in this chapter:

- How your decisions about your future shape how to make your business saleable today.

- Why answering five critical questions is essential to forming the goals that will motivate you throughout the remaining steps.

- How a valuation growth lever can help you see how to become worth what you want to sell the business for.

Step 2 - Hone Goals and Decisions

Your next step in building your Saleability Blueprint is to hone your goals and decisions. It's time to look forward.

There are many decisions you have to make. You can't make a great decision without first setting your goal and your desired end result. Consider the following questions, and see if you can begin to answer them.

These four important decisions set you on your journey to becoming saleable:

1. When do you want to exit?

2. How much do you want your company to be worth upon exit?

3. What will you move on to when you've left your company?

4. What kind of legacy do you want to leave?

These four decisions are intertwined. In your intention to come to conclusions about what's important to you in each question, you have to consider the other questions hand in hand.

For instance, to answer the question "When do you want to exit?" (question 1.), you will want to understand the amount of work involved in getting your company to the value you want to be able to sell it for (question 2.).

Simultaneously, you need to do your market research on who your ideal buyer is in order to be able to get closer to a specific date by which you want to have your business ready for sale. You may remember that buyers are looking when it suits them to look and not when it suits you, as the father and son business story revealed.

It is hard for any of us to know when we are at the top of our game, the peak of the growth curve, or the cusp of an industry disruption or economic disturbance. Being ready sooner allows you to surf with these uncontrollable variables. We all wish we had predicted when a public company stock reached its highest value and sold the day before the price started its downward trajectory.

Hindsight is always 20/20, as the old adage goes, but don't let your mind wander to that old saw. The right aphorism to remember in this case is that opportunity rewards the prepared.

To motivate yourself to want to exit at a certain date, you have to be excited about pursuing your next act.

In order to fund your next act (question 3.), you will want your company to be worth the amount that will keep you going in the manner in which you have been accustomed.

If you want to sell for thousands or millions more than the number in your baseline, "back of the napkin" calculation, then you have to be willing to make changes. Being open and adaptable to change is not for everyone. You may have to change your role, how you lead, fix long-standing problems that you have managed in a way that has now become a barrier to growth, share information you have held tight in the past, or let go of nonperforming employees, products, services, messages, branding, or other elements that all flash red flags to buyers.

To motivate yourself to make your company saleable by your desired exit date (question 1.), you will have to be moving toward a future you look forward to. Otherwise, you won't make the effort or set the priority to do the work of making your business saleable. Instead, you will want to envision your company flourishing on into the future under new owners. This exploration helps you let go. It helps you see your business as serving the greater good. When you work for this result, all your stakeholders and your local economy are rewarded… or, to put it another way, they don't lose out in the long run. At some point in the not-so-distant future, an un-saleable company starts to shed employees, suppliers, and customers as growth slows and value shrinks. Instead, envision deep satisfaction for all concerned. Because of your decision to make your business saleable so that it attracts some of that ten trillion dollars looking for saleable companies, your influence helps all boats rise. Imagine the pride you will feel knowing that your choices helped to take care of everyone's future in a way that makes you a real hero.

How to Envision Your Next Act

Most people like to look forward to things in life. Business owners who've owned their companies for a long time can find it hard to see themselves doing anything else. You are moving toward a new stage of your life that will come with a new identity, activities, people, groups, and fulfillment.

Take a moment and imagine yourself free of your daily routine. There are no meetings to go to. You can do whatever you want. Many people, after years of structure, fall into one of two camps: they either need a new structure; or they are ready to break free of structure.

You know yourself. The more structure you think you need, the more you will want to plan out how you will embark on your new life and start a new venture – perhaps working with charities, serving on boards, or cheering on your kids and grandkids at their events. We continually recreate ourselves, so if you anticipate feeling a void, then begin to envision what you will create for yourself post exit.

If you are sick of structure, then give yourself a break. Plan an adventure. Spend a year doing whatever you feel like doing. Let yourself be inspired by freedom of choice and a wealth of new opportunity.

Just make sure you talk to your financial planner about what that freeform adventure or structured plan will cost you. You want to make sure your wealth nest egg from selling your company can support your choice.

Got Partners? Get Them Involved

These four critical decisions can't be made in a vacuum. Even if you are a solo owner, you absolutely need to get your best friend, a trusted advisor, or family involved in this next step. Your partners and family members will need to take these same steps in order to be able to start having real conversations about selling and not just the "We'll sell the company one day…" discussion that leads nowhere.

1.   When do you want to exit?

2.   How much do you want your company to be worth upon exit?

3.   What will you move on to when you've left your company?

4.   What kind of legacy do you want to leave?

How to Get Partners and Stakeholders to Answer these Questions

PHASE 1. Call a meeting with your partners or, if you're a solo owner, with your spouse and friends. This is no time to go it alone. Hand out copies of this book. Describe what you have just learned about what it takes to make a company saleable.

PHASE 2. On a white board, list the four critical questions. Then, say that you will have a discussion about everyone's needs. They will all be heard. Next, find out if people have thought about these questions and get their early thoughts written down. Their answers will change as you progress through your discussions. It's vital that you, as the leader, capture their interests so that they feel heard. You know more than they do at this point. So, suspend your judgment as you listen and write. Your goal in taking this step is to get the conversation going, not to have the decision made. Eye rolling, cracking jokes, sighing, and snide remarks squash discussion. In fact, it sets up an atmosphere where stakeholders don't want to have any kind of conversation, never mind plan out how everyone will get the biggest payday of their lives. If you are worried about how this step will go, then retain a facilitator to manage the interaction.

PHASE 3. On the white board, write down the valuation range from lowest to highest from the answers to question two. Calculate the difference between the lowest and highest number in the range.

PHASE 4. Post the company's "back of the napkin," unofficial valuation number we just helped you calculate in the last step.

PHASE 5. Now calculate the differences between both the bottom and top ends of the range and your valuation number. The result is called your Opportunity Gap. To be able to sell when you want, for what you want, you have to close your opportunity gap. Your opportunity gap is the amount by which you want to increase your company's value. You will shortly learn about the valuation growth levers that will help you accomplish this step.

PHASE 6. Now let's validate the size of the range and the opportunity gap. The top end of the range is what everyone wants to sell it for, but is the opportunity gap closable or is it too wide? Now write the Multiple number on the white board using the valuation calculator that your industry is getting on deals that close.

PHASE 7. Divide both the low and high end of the range by that Multiple. The result is what your Earnings Before Interest, Tax, Depreciation, and Amortization have to grow to.

PHASE 8. You should also calculate what percentage this number is of your current gross sales or revenue – Desired Earnings Before Interest and Tax divided by Current Sales. This is your profit margin goal. Then, calculate your current profit margin: Current Earnings Before Interest and Tax divided by Current Sales. How much are you expecting to grow your profit margin by in order to meet your valuation goal?

If the earnings needed to close the opportunity gap seem un-achievable, then you may have to scale back your expectations or work on a longer-term growth strategy that will take longer than two to four years. You will want to understand how to use your valuation growth levers in your business. Read on for an explanation on what a valuation growth lever is.

Valuation Growth Levers

You learned that adding green lights and fixing red flags is how you increase your Multiple from the baseline of three times EBITDA. You are now going to learn how to increase your valuation. Below is an example to help you understand the relationship between sales growth, EBITDA growth, and Multiple growth. These are your three growth levers. To get the valuation you are aiming for, you can make adjustments in your strategy on any of these three levers or on all of them depending on how big the spread (your opportunity gap) is between your baseline valuation and what you want to sell your company for.

In the example in Figure 7, look at the left-hand column first. Today, this company has twenty million dollars in sales with a 7% of sales EBITDA. We give them a baseline Multiple of 3 be-cause the company is un-saleable. On paper, they are worth $4.2 million. This company is in an industry where profit margins for saleable companies are 9% or more. This is one of several reasons why this business is un-saleable.

From Un-Saleable to Saleable
Close Your Opportunity Gap

Today	Millions	%		2 Years	Millions	%
Revenues	$20	100%		Revenues	$20	100%
EBITDA	$ 1.4	**7%**		EBITDA	$ 2	**10%**
Multiple	**3X**			Multiple	**4X**	
Today's Value		$ 4.2		**Value in 2 Years**		$ 8
Valuation Goal		$ 8		Valuation Goal		$ 8
Valuation Gap		$3.8		Valuation Gap		$ 0
Saleable ?		No		Saleable?		Yes

Figure 7 – From Un-saleable to Saleable

To become saleable, they have to fix that profitability red flag and use their EBITDA valuation lever to grow the margin to at least 9%. The owners determine that growing sales might be difficult. So, instead, they set goals to reach a higher Multiple by adding green lights. Their industry-comparable Multiple is fairly low since their business is based on winning projects, which creates risk in future cash flow.

So, they commit to making their company saleable by making the changes inside their business within the next two years that make it worth what they want to sell it for, which is eight million dollars.

How do they do that?

1. **Sales Lever:** The owners will need to ensure they at least hold sales steady.

2. **EBITDA Lever:** They tighten up how they spend

to produce their product, project, or service so that they get growth in their gross margin (sales minus cost of goods sold or direct labor). They might also need to pay attention to fixed costs. By holding these costs steady or even finding some reductions, all the extra that was gained in the gross margin goes straight to the EBITDA number. This is how this particular company grew EBITDA from a below industry average of 7% to 10% of sales.

3. **Multiple Lever:** In their industry, buyers pay close attention to service revenues, which are favored over project revenues. This company focused on winning more service and maintenance contracts on each new project they installed, as well as searching for opportunities to win business away from competitors. They widened the number of offerings in their service contracts and bundled them together, increasing prices by a barely noticeable 2%. Collectively, these strategies strengthened the value of each contract. This additional sales revenue counterbalanced the uncertainty of knowing whether they would be the successful bidders in any new projects. They also created better reporting and accountability in tracking the success of each project so that they could fix any problems that would delay billing or profitability before they spiraled out of control. These adjustments stabilized the sales number but didn't add to growth. However, against their competitors, these changes made them far more attractive to their ideal buyers (larger contracting firms moving into this geographic market), which increased the Multiple from 3 to 4.

Imagine growing the value of your business by 47% from an unsaleable valuation of $4.2 million to a saleable valuation of $8 million in just two years!

So, let's return to the meeting you are leading with your partners and stakeholders. You've just finished taking them through the Valuation Growth Levers exercise. Now, it's time for the next step.

PHASE 9. You've delivered a lot of mind-boggling information about the potential future you and your fellow shareholders and stakeholders could enjoy. Now, you need to hear from them. Ask them for their observations, concerns, questions, and reflections, and write down what they say. Again, suspend your judgment.

I strongly suggest that you photograph or capture the notes you take so you have them to refer to in your next meeting. Before you close the meeting, ask everyone to read this book you are now holding in your hands and *Fast-Track Secrets for Making Your Business Saleable*. Set a date and time for your next meeting when everyone will have had a chance to digest this news and come to terms with what is important to them.

PHASE 10. Your next step is to meet with your spouse, friend, or life coach to determine what you want to do next in your life. We call this your "next act." It might not mean retirement. It might be something you've always wanted to do. Then, meet with a financial planner to talk about how much money you will need to fund your new chosen lifestyle.

PHASE 11. It's time to bring everyone back together again now that they have had time to read the books and think about what they've learned and how it will impact their own interests and goals. Post the same four questions on the board. Create two columns next to the questions. The first column is for the answers from the previous meeting. The second column will be to record any changes to their previous answers.

After everyone has contributed their thoughts and observations, as well as answered each question, it is time to ask the fifth and final question that completes Step 2 – Hone Goals and Decisions:

"Are we committed to doing the work to make this company saleable?"

If the answer is yes, then go back to your exit date and make sure you have an achievable date with enough time to make the changes. Evaluate when the optimum time is for your company to be put on the market. Ideally, you want it to be before its peak.

By answering yes to this question, it means you and your partners are committing to learning how to use your valuation growth levers inside your business so that it is worth what you want when you want to sell it.

If you answered no, then you have another choice to make: Do you continue on as you are and be satisfied with the level of income you have with your lifestyle business; or Do you bring in a General Manager to do the work of making your business saleable? Whichever route you take, you can still benefit from doing some of the things I am showing you here...so keep reading.

PHASE 12. Now, review the exit value. Adjust for any expectations that have changed. You may need to narrow the range, depending on the growth goals you have set for yourselves.

PHASE 13. After reviewing your options to grow the Sales, EBITDA, and/or the Multiple, you now need to examine the gaps between current values and what you need your numbers to become. Use your best judgment and experience to evaluate the reality of achieving that growth. Using the left hand column of the model in Figure 7, which is shown again on the following page for your reference, plug in your sales number from last year, then your EBITDA number and the Multiple of 3.

From Un-Saleable to Saleable
Close Your Opportunity Gap

Today	Millions	%		2 Years	Millions	%
Revenues	$20	100%		Revenues	$20	100%
EBITDA	$ 1.4	**7%**		EBITDA	$ 2	**10%**
Multiple	**3X**			Multiple	**4X**	
Today's Value		**$ 4.2**		**Value in 2 Years**		**$ 8**
Valuation Goal		$ 8		Valuation Goal		$ 8
Valuation Gap		$3.8		Valuation Gap		$ 0
Saleable ?		No		Saleable?		Yes

Figure 7 – From Un-saleable to Saleable

Now, using the right hand column, run the numbers for any of your selected exit dates. What would happen if you wanted to sell within two years? What about four years?

How much would sales have to grow by? Calculate the percentage.

How about EBITDA? Look at your industry's Multiples. If your company's Multiple is at a baseline of 3 times EBITDA now and other companies are selling between 8 times and 10 times, then you may have to add many more green lights to your business than our example company had to do.

Think about which green lights are important by referring to Figure 6 - The Multiple Effect. How long will it take you to add some of these features?

This kind of "What if ?" scenario planning helps you to break down the effort involved in getting to your valuation goals. Expect that as you learn how to narrow down who your best acquirer will be during Step 3 – Hunt the Right Acquirer, your scenarios will change and become more fine-tuned. This is the work of building a Saleability Blueprint.

As you go through all these scenarios, make sure you have a lengthy discussion for each one. What will it take operationally to achieve this growth? What has to change about how you currently track your numbers so that you can keep track of the metrics? Who do you need to consult with to help you answer these questions effectively? Let your accountant in on your plans so that he or she can help you upgrade your software system and get better decision-making data. Talk to your banker about better cash-management strategies so that you aren't leaning on your credit line. After thorough discussion and careful planning, you know what benchmarks you're going to have to hit inside your business in order for it to become saleable.

Chapter 5 Summary

Below are the key takeaways from this chapter. Did you miss any? If so, go back and re-read the chapter because these concepts are essential to truly understanding Step 3 – Hunt the Right Acquirer.

- There are five critical questions that need answers so that you can know where you are going, by when, and what you have to do to get there so you can make a commitment to making your business saleable.

- There are three valuation levers that can be used to increase the value of your company and make it saleable.

- It is essential that you educate your partners and any stakeholders who care about what happens to the value of your business. Facilitate a meeting where you capture their interests and compare them with your own so that you all agree on your goals.

The answers to these questions are essential to know how to identify the ideal acquirer for your business which is the third step to becoming saleable that we will cover in the next chapter.

CHAPTER 6

BECOME WHAT YOUR IDEAL BUYER NEEDS

W hat you will learn in this chapter:

- What makes for an ideal acquirer.

- How your idea of the ideal acquirer might not fit with the reality of your business situation, your personal goals, and the expectations you and your stakeholders have about your options for business growth.

- How to evaluate and select the best-fit acquirer.

Step 3: Hunt The Right Acquirer

Once you know your own goals, you are ready to learn how to look at your business as a buyer does. You will want to transform your company into what your ideal acquirer would want; into what they are looking for you to have. Before you do that, you have to select what is the likely ideal type of buyer. I don't mean that you have to name the company or person who will buy your company one day.

I mean for you to identify the type of buyer who would more than likely find your company exactly what they are looking for. Your company should fill the buyer's needs, just like your customers or clients look to your business to fill their needs. They pick your company to do business with over any others for some key reasons. The buyer will do the same. When you are ready for sale down the road, your M&A advisor or business broker will do the work of making the connection to specific buyers within your ideal buyer category.

At this stage, we want to discover the key reasons a buyer category would be ideal for you. When a buyer looks at your company, they don't see what you see. They look for the green lights that tell them that your company will continue to return a profit if they buy it.

Each buyer has their own reasons for buying. There are several types of buyers:

Strategic buyers are companies searching for acquisitions that:

- Help them grow

- Reduce costs

- Reduce risks

- Expand into new markets

- Get better economies of scale

- Expand cash flow

- Acquire a higher volume of transactions to offset fixed costs

- Add another feature to products and services

- Expand to adjacent markets or offset cyclical industry risk by buying a company that works in a counter cycle

- Acquire new technology or patents

- Create a better brand or marketing strategy

Financial buyers, often known as "private equity groups," have similar interests to those of strategic buyers with one key exception. They have raised money based on a specific return guarantee to the people and institutions who invested with them. Therefore, they have much narrower criteria for what makes an acquisition ideal.

Independent Buyers want healthy cash flow and to grow cash flow.

Entrepreneurs, immigrant investors, employees, and family members may be buying a lifestyle job, fulfilling a dream, or acquiring that potential for a winning ticket that could fund their future. They need to be able to use the company's cash flow to finance the buyout, which means that your company has to meet the lender's criteria of strong cash flow to pay back the loan.

Selling to Your Employees

Did you know that United Airlines is owned by its employees under an ESOP, an Employee Stock Ownership Plan? In the U.S., this practice is becoming more popular for company owners. It has certain tax advantages and can be a handsome reward for the employees that helped you get to where you are today… able to claim a return on your investment in your business. You may want to explore this option with an expert in structuring ESOPs to see if your business might qualify.

Selling to Management or a General Manager

Many owners are realizing that to gain back life balance and have more freedom or to grow to the next level, they need someone to lead the business on their behalf. Recognize that growing a business to the level it needs to be to become saleable is both a painful moment and an exciting new evolution in the future of your business. An experienced GM is often what buyers are looking for because you should not have a functional role in the company by the time you're ready to entertain buyers.

A management buyout requires several years of planning and still more to complete your earn-out. Learn what is involved before you set your sights on this type of buyer.

How Do You Know Which Buyer to Select?

To make the right buyer selection, you will have to do some research. If you know you have employees (or family members or an entrepreneur) who want to buy into the company and they will be comfortable taking on the risk of putting in at least ten percent of their own equity and can also drive business growth so the company becomes a cash flow machine, then there is only one question left for you. Are you willing to be tied to the business for five to seven years until your payout is complete?

Ninety percent of acquisitions are made by strategic buyers. If your company is a small fish in a big pond, then you may be able to become part of a larger company's industry consolidation or growth strategy. Your research on Google, Yahoo! Finance, at your industry association, and through talking to your suppliers will help you uncover which companies are buying and the types of deals they are making.

Don't Make This Mistake!

While it might be tempting to keep your options open, it will actually derail your saleability plan. Make the choice of the type of buyer you will eventually sell to before you take the next step to helm the transition.

It can take years to build up the cash flow that enables an employee to buy you out. On the other hand, you could sell much more quickly to a strategic buyer but only if you've modeled your company to become what they need to acquire.

It is essential that you set yourself up to be the best fit for the best buyer. Just remember, you have to build a plan for the previous two steps before you are ready to determine your best acquirer.

Chapter 6 Summary

Here are the takeaways from this chapter:

- There are many buyer types. Only a few or maybe even one will be most suitable for your business.

- Do the research to learn what you need to in order to determine which type of buyer might be the best fit for your company.

- Before you take Step 4 – Helm the Transition, realize that you have to commit to one type of buyer, which could be seen as a risk by some owners. But, failing to commit to one path makes your business UN-saleable to any buyer type, and that is a far greater risk.

CHAPTER 7

FIND WHAT MAKES YOUR BUSINESS SALEABLE AND UN-SALEABLE

W e've reached the final step in making your business Saleable. This is what you will learn in this chapter:

- Most businesses have red flags that make buyers move on to the next opportunity. These same red flags also cause you, the current owner, problems. Finding them and fixing them is in your best interests.

- Green lights are what buyers search for as these are the elements that will enable them to reach their growth goals. Adding the right green lights will help you reach your growth goals, too.

- Determine which red flags lurk in your business and which green lights will make a big difference in your operations.

Step 4: Helm the Transition

Fix the Red Flags and Add the Green Lights

The fourth step in building your custom Saleability Blueprint is to helm the transition. In this step, you will learn how to see the red flags that buyers can spot at ten paces and understand what kinds of green lights you will need in order to attract your ideal buyer.

As you learn about what doesn't work in your business, there is a temptation to leap into action to fix these issues immediately.

Please don't. First, what you change might just be a Band-Aid over a much larger symptom that you have yet to uncover. Your efforts could confuse the situation at best or, at worst, set you in a direction from which it is hard to recover. It is wasted time, effort, and money to act without a full understanding of all the changes that will help fix the red flags you encounter.

Secondly, the solution you decide upon should be based on what your ideal buyer would most like to see, rather than on the popular idea offered up by you or the management team.

Every profitability leak that we've encountered has roots in other problems and multiple departments. However, we all like to think that the problem sits with one person or one department and that there is one solution. This is rarely the case.

To build that plan, learn to see the green lights and red flags in your company just as buyers and investors do.

Let's look at some of the typical buyer green lights, those sale-ability factors we referred to with respect to the Multiple. Green lights are subjective. Strategic buyers search for their "green light" perfect fit. Financial buyers want cash flow and growth prospects. Lenders look for the same green lights as financial buyers when considering lending for growth and/or a partial equity buyout or management buyout.

As we go through the green light list – the buyer acquisition criteria – realize that most companies only have a few green lights...

and this is the key reason why most businesses aren't saleable.

Only having a few green lights in accordance with buyer perspective does not mean you and your company are not successful. It is, in fact, fairly typical because most owners operate their companies for their own benefit and not for the benefit of the next owner, at least not yet.

Below are some examples of green lights potential buyers will want to see. They don't need to see all of them, but there should be enough that they get that little adrenaline rush that tells them your company is worth investigating.

Check all that you have set up in your company:

- ❑   Realistic, rosy future forecast
- ❑   Not dependent on owner
- ❑   Effective management team
- ❑   Profitability leaks plugged
- ❑   Systems that allow scalability
- ❑   Vision, goals, metrics, plans
- ❑   Consistently profitable in the previous two years

Now, if you are like most business owners in this stage of the process, then you can confidently check off two or three of these attributes. The rest come as a direct result of building your four-step plan for making your business saleable and from leading your company through the changes your plan lays out. So, don't be too hard on yourself if you've only ticked a few boxes. This exercise helps you see what has to be done; you are continually handling reality.

Typical Red Flags That Lower the Multiple

When a buyer spots a red flag, they start to discount the value of buying the company. Too many and your company doesn't even get an exploratory phone call. If the buyer uncovers red flags during due diligence after they have made an offer in a Letter of Intent (LOI), then the chances are that this discovery will affect the Multiple they are willing to offer.

At this point, they may lower the Multiple, which will affect the offer number or result in the withdrawal of the LOI entirely. This event could happen regardless of how much time they have invested in getting to know your company and how much time you have invested in entertaining their questions (typically months).

This is the critical inside information that we spent years gleaning from the minds of buyers. Know your red flags long before taking a call from a buyer.

This is not a complete list, but buyers know how to spot all of these red flags, and it stops them in their tracks. In fact, these are the issues that contribute to the statistic we described earlier – the reason why 90% of business owners either fail to find a buyer or fall short of closing the deal.

As we go through the list, check off the ones you think may exist in your company:

- ❑ Profitability leaks.
- ❑ Unclear roles and responsibilities.
- ❑ Owner is needed in the business.
- ❑ Senior personnel do admin/clerical work.
- ❑ Customer base is concentrated.

❏ Company is reactive to market forces.

❏ Inconsistent decision-making references.

❏ Owner makes all the decisions.

❏ Data and insight unavailable to adequately explain why margins fluctuate across product or service lines.

❏ Owner believes the buyer's offer does not represent the company's value and uses history as evidence rather than a future growth plan.

❏ The company has not achieved consistent year-over-year growth. Sales are stagnant or slow.

❏ The company does not have a written plan about how it will achieve growth.

❏ The company is not a standout in its market niche.

❏ The company operates very similarly to its competitors.

❏ Prices are often discounted to achieve a sale.

❏ Company knowledge, processes, or procedures are not captured and made accessible to employees who need it.

❏ There is no history of plans that were made and what was achieved that can tell the story of how the company gets results.

This list can be daunting to read if you find yourself checking more than a few boxes. Having more than a few red flags is fairly typical of even much larger companies than yours. Still, these issues do have to be remedied. Let's explore what we mean by some of these red flags so that you can better understand their role and the measure of their impact in your company.

Do you have profitability leaks?

To decide where to invest growth capital, it is essential to know which products, services, and solutions make the company have the greatest margin.

If you can't see into your business through this lens, then you may need a financial analyst to help you prepare new reporting systems that reveal what is really happening under the hood.

Pricing strategy is often a source of leaks. Owners are hesitant to put prices up because they think they will lose the sale. We all have a bias toward big round numbers. Think one or two percent – hardly noticeable except to your EBITDA.

Are you financing your customers? Invoicing and billing may have to be overhauled so that you get your money sooner.

Do sales people provide discounts in the belief that this is what will close the sale? They need training on how to sell value, not price, and on how to solve problems, not negotiate pricing.

Have you reviewed what it really costs to get your product out the door lately? You may discover extra labor and double activity of which you weren't aware.

We know there are unclear roles and responsibilities when:

- ❑ The owners do not have job descriptions.

- ❑ There are frequent conflicts between departments about who is supposed to do what and when and how information is supposed to flow amongst departments.

- ❑ People have job descriptions that don't match what

they actually do.

- ❑ On any given day, there is a line of people at the owner's door who need to be told whether or not they can do something or how to solve a problem.

We know that senior personnel are doing admin work when:

- ❑ They are dealing with their own inbox and doing their own research.

- ❑ They don't have specific agendas for the meetings they attend.

- ❑ They aren't spending at least twenty percent of their day on pushing the strategic plan forward.

Additional Red Flags

- ❑ A concentrated customer base is where the company is dependent on any one client or customer to provide more than twenty percent of total revenue or sales.

- ❑ A company that is reactive to market forces does not have or follow an action plan to become known as the "go-to" company or brand for something a specific market niche hungers for.

- ❑ A company that uses inconsistent decision-making references has no useful reporting or metrics system to help know what works and what doesn't. Another indicator is the existence of regular conflicts about who is right and who is wrong rather than there being discussion to fully understand the root of the problem and what needs to be done to gain momentum and traction.

❑ And now for the biggest red flag buyers run from: The business owner insists his or her company is worth more than the buyer decides it's worth.

The owner who has not uncovered these red flags and has not built an integrated plan to resolve them doesn't have a saleable company. A buyer can't purchase a company with lots of red flags; the investment would be too risky. So, to the buyer, the company does not have value. This is a critical distinction that business owners struggle to come to terms with. Value is in the mind of the buyer, not the owner.

Time to take a deep breath. Like many business owners, you may have mentally checked off many more boxes on the red flag list than the green lights list. Again, don't worry; this is typical, but you can work to become part of that atypical, saleable 10%.

Once you understand what needs to change inside your business, first fix these red flags, which we call "stabilization." Then, add in the green lights in the right sequence, which forms part of your growth strategy, and you will be helming the right changes.

I'm often asked how the ideal buyer will be found. We've seen this happen several times in our consulting practice with our clients. They make their decisions, focus their efforts on strategic buyers, and start implementing their Saleability Blueprints.

Then, seemingly out of the blue, they get a phone call from one of several ideal buyers in their industry.

What you might not know about strategic and financial buyers is that they have teams of people monitoring every industry they are interested in. They know which companies are up and coming, which are winning market share, which are gaining reputations for stellar service, gold star products, and innovations that make life easier, and which are solving real world problems in a way that customers love.

Your business will be found when you have made your mark.

What about independent buyers? They are harder to meet. They often visit business brokers, so there will come a time when you will want to make it known your business is for sale.

If your ideal buyer is within your internal environment, then the time to start talking is now. If you think your son or daughter or employee is the right person to own your business, then your first step is to find out if this is something they want. Don't let their answer affect your view of them. Taking on the financial risk that buying your company will entail is not for everyone, as much as they may like the business and appreciate your offer. This is not a situation that you should take personally. Your legacy and your relationships only suffer if you decide to take offense when the person declines.

Making the changes to your operation may require the services of a seasoned consultant or analyst to help you hunt down the root causes of those red flags and develop a solution that works for your ideal buyer.

You may also need coaching in changing how you lead. The owners we work with have had to learn how to stop taking over and start delegating in a way that sets up their managers for success, not failure. Letting go of this need for control can be hard to do as we noted in Step 1 - Handle Reality where the owner made the commitment, but his behavior exposed his unwillingness to trust his employees.

Don't underestimate the amount of personal change you may have to make in terms of your attitude and what you spend your time on. We know another owner who really didn't like coming up with the plans for his various departments. He knew that strategic planning was not his strength. Yet, he had hired people to work for him who were very tactical. They came up with great plans that solved problems that didn't seem to drive the business forward in any meaningful way. Asking them for more strategic plans didn't help because they didn't know the difference.

Each of his red flags required a solution that would solve the problem for the whole company, not just the department they led. Having to work with their peers on larger and more interdependent issues was beyond their ability.

He struggled with his team until he realized what he really wanted were more sophisticated managers leading his departments, which meant he would have to hire people to replace the people he had come to trust. It was a hard transition for him until he found three people who could think and plan strategically and implement tactically.

Soon, he was able to have four-day and then two-day work weeks. When a buyer saw that his team was capable of leading the company through the stabilization work (fixing those red flags), they had the confidence to offer him a number with which he was very satisfied.

What will your challenges be in leading the changes necessary with Step 4 – Helm the Transition? Check the boxes below that you feel may prove to be difficult.

- ❑ Find the red flags.

- ❑ Analyze the root cause of why they exist.

- ❑ See how the root cause affects other areas of the business.

- ❑ Develop a plan to come up with the best solution.

- ❑ Get employees to come up with the best solution.

❑ Find the time to form a team that knows how to implement the plan on top of regular functional responsibilities.

❑ Evaluate whether the solution chosen is actually solving the right problem in the best way for the long-term needs of the company.

❑ Coach employees on how to develop and implement a plan.

❑ Set up metrics to track progress on achieving results.

❑ Manage the team and follow up to make sure the plan is progressing.

❑ Acknowledge the work done.

Consider that if you have checked any of these boxes, then you may want to find a consultant or coach who can help you turn these red flag fixes into projects and help you lead or delegate the projects in a way that works for all.

Coming to Terms with What You Have Learned

In this book, I wanted to show you the power you have in your hands just by making a few critical decisions. By following our proven four-step system, which builds your Saleability Blueprint, you will be ready to helm the transition. You will helm the transition by changing what you need to inside your business so that it is better for you financially and operationally, as well as being appealing to a buyer.

I won't pretend there's not a steep learning curve to seeing your business the way buyers do. However, you aren't exactly afraid of challenges; you started your business and became part of the small percentage of entrepreneurs who succeeded. Now, you can position your business and yourself so you win the final reward – a buyer willing to pay you the value you want to sell your business for.

The good news before you right now is that you have already begun to identify some of the concrete steps you can take in order to join the 10% who have business sales success stories.

You are at a fork in the road. Which direction will you take?

Will you leave your future to chance?

Or...

Will you learn how to build your own Saleability Blueprint, customized for your business situation so that you will have far greater certainty that you will be able to sell your business for what you want, when you want, and thus claim your wealth?

- ❑ Yes, I want to do the work to become Saleable. I want a return on my investment.

- ❑ No, I don't think I will be selling my business. I will close it down when I'm ready to retire or move on to something else.

- ❑ No, I think my business is successful enough as it is and I will take my chances selling it when I'm ready to deal with exiting. Right now, I'm just too busy to think about the future.

If you answered yes, then you need a Saleability Blueprint. We have the resources to help you build it.

Good News

It is possible to make most businesses Saleable (and more profitable in the meantime, which rewards you!) and, as a result, attract a buyer who wants exactly what you have and is willing to pay you a premium. It just takes having the right plan, some commitment, some effort, and some focus… but the rewards can be truly stunning when you get it right.

Chapter 7 Summary

Here are the takeaways from learning about how to helm the transition:

- You now know which green lights you may want to add to your business to make it easier to run, more profitable, and more appealing to your ideal buyer.

- You understand the power of red flags to make a company un-saleable and realize you want to find and fix these issues so they make your business more successful for you.

- You understand that you don't make changes inside your business until you've completed your Saleability Blueprint.

- There may be personal and professional changes you need to make in regards to how you lead and manage.

- Depending on your realistic assessment of your strengths, you may need a consultant, coach, or analyst to help you helm the transition.

CHAPTER 8

SO IS THIS SALEABILITY EFFORT WORTH IT?

What you will learn in this chapter:

- What it takes to make the changes inside the company.

- How one company managed the tricky process of gaining agreement and buy-in from all the owners.

- What this business did to get their desired end result.

Let's remind ourselves of the facts. Currently, only 10% of owners get to the finish line. If you can't sell your company, then what will you do with it? The impacts of not selling affect you, your family, your employees, customers, suppliers, your town, and your industry.

When the company's wealth diminishes, so does everyone else's. So, what matters to you? Getting in that 10%? Making sure you aren't trying to drive your company when you've lost the juice? Leaving a legacy that rewards everyone in your business and family?

Let's look at one of our case studies. When we first met these owners, they had only two green lights out of nine and had twelve out of fourteen red flags. Our "back of the napkin" valuation placed their value between $9m and $10m, which means their EBITDA was about $3m despite the fact that sales had grown to $37m. Their growth strategy had paid off, but their operation was burning through cash. Their industry competitors who managed to sell their companies had profit margins closer to 12%, not 8%. Although they had enjoyed 20% growth, it was driven more by economic factors rather than any particular market share, niche, or secret sauce they employed.

This company had two big red flags: no competitive advantage and no ability to control costs. Each of these red flags had many tentacles spanning the entire company. It would be complex to uncover the root causes and remedy them with smart solutions.

To say that the owners of this company were frustrated despite the fact that everyone else was applauding their growth in sales would be an understatement.

They wanted out in two years. Yet, they were inconsistently profitable and not just because of the economy. They had profitability leaks, and they didn't know where to look to find them. They had grown a successful company. They did great work. Their customers loved them.

So, they did something many business owners aren't willing to do. Together with their spouses and families, they made a big decision. They committed to learning how to become saleable, to making the right changes in their business, to transforming it into what a strategic buyer would want. They wanted that big payout and realized all they had to do was to make that commitment.

In less than two years after learning how to stabilize their company by fixing those leaks, they were fielding calls from several strategic buyers. They weren't quite ready for a buyer though.

They were still in the stability stage of their Saleability Blueprint. They had learned that they couldn't start growing without first stabilizing. So, the partners said thanks but no thanks.

Despite that brush off, one strategic buyer kept returning to visit. They wanted to acquire the distribution relationships in a sector they couldn't get into on their own. Our client had those relationships.

Over the course of a year, the strategic buyer witnessed the changes the company was making. After that "getting to know you" year, the strategic buyer made an offer. They suggested that the owners could sell now. If their cost control plan and growth strategy to become the "go-to" company in the niche to which the buyer wanted access would pay off within a two-year time-frame, then the owners would receive their full valuation request. However, it would be broken into three parts. The first part was a lump-sum payment up front. Two-thirds of the price would be paid upon closing. Then, the second and third payments would be made when the company achieved the metrics they claimed they could achieve.

This deal is called an earn-out. It is a very respectable and fair way to help the seller get the full value of the success of the Sale-ability Blueprint and a way for the buyer to mitigate the risk that the management team won't be able to gain the necessary growth in the business.

The Turning Point

I remember the day the offer came in. All eyes were riveted on that binder as it sat on their boardroom table. The partners turned to the page with the offering number, and there it was in black and white: the number they and their spouses had agreed on twenty-four months prior.

Suddenly, it sank in. The families had earned their return on their investment. It was a truly breathtaking moment to watch their transformation. With the stroke of a pen (and twenty-four months of elbow grease), they had secured their families' wealth. They were securing their employees' futures. They were solidifying their legacy after the years spent driving this company from a forty-person minor player in an overcrowded market to a one hundred-seventy-person company being acquired by a blue-chip firm, selected over top of many others.

This is what they did. They grew all their saleability levers: Sales by one percent, EBITDA by four percent, and the Multiple by two times, and they did this by becoming the "go-to" company in the industry to which the acquirer wanted access.

Additionally, they learned how to invest their wealth so that they could safely live off the income it produces, rather than the salary they don't have any more.

Will You Get Similar Results if You Build and Implement Your Saleability Blueprint?

It's true that not every business is in the kind of industry that attracts premium acquisitions. Not every company is going to find a strategic buyer that is consolidating the industry by rolling up smaller companies. Not every business has an obvious ideal buyer.

If you want to find out more about which buyer will suit your company and how to get started building your Saleability Blueprint and your plans for each of the four steps, then I'll tell you how to get thirty minutes on the phone with me personally. You can contact us at http://www.spiritwest.com/schedule-a-30-min-call/ to arrange your private and confidential appointment. Just reference this book.

You are probably wondering if there is a catch here.

Our system works for one reason and one reason only: the business owners that we work with are committed to getting their desired end result. In fact, they are passionate about making these changes. These people are inspiring to be around.

They are willing to learn, to change, to look themselves in the eye and face reality. We can't do a darn thing for an owner who doesn't want to make the changes we suggest. Nothing.

You should know what gets in the way of making your company saleable. These are the roadblocks that owners often face. Luckily, they are all easy to move through but require making new decisions:

1. **Limited Time** When will you have time to do all this work? Many owners live in a world where time is the enemy. There is never enough, and it's always running out. We call this "scarcity thinking." What it really says is that you are not able to prioritize what is important, and so, you are trying to do everything. That lack of focus is what is causing time scarcity, and it is often the tone that is set inside the company so people's level of anxiety is high and things never seem to get done. This mindset is debilitating and causes enormous stress. You need to think about the results you really want and not about how much time everything takes. Those people who succeed at getting to the finish line don't work longer hours. They think about the actions that drive value, and their decisions follow suit. They spend their time on their strengths and priorities and learn how to delegate and mentor

other people to do the rest.

2. **How Long is this Work Going to Take? I Want to Sell Sooner, not Later.** If you are just discovering this book in the year that you thought you would sell, either by choice or circumstance, then I do have compassion for you. You could attempt to sell now but then recognize that it might be impossible after consuming a huge amount of your time, hope, and energy. Alternatively, you could build your Saleability Blueprint now, identify your best hope for a buyer in the shortest possible timeframe (probably not an independent or internal buyer), and then make a few key changes that at least increase the probability that your business would be saleable. Check with a business broker now to see what they believe the probability is that you would find a buyer.

3. **My Partners and I are at Different Stages of our Lives. They Won't Agree to Sell.** You may still be able to sell a minority interest in the business to a private equity group or ask your partners to buy you out. However, before you hope that they would be willing to consider other options, it would be wise to suggest that everyone read this book. Then, facilitate the planning session we suggested for bringing partners together. You may be surprised what a little knowledge does for closed minds. Remember, you don't have to wait for other people to change. You lead the way by suggesting that you all learn how to get a return on your investment and then watch how this new information changes the way your partners talk about an exit.

What you need to do is be the ripple of change yourself. Decide to start learning how to make your business saleable even if your partners aren't on the same page about it. Share what you are learning. Don't push for a decision on a date or value number until you've gone through that process yourself.

It all boils down to what future you want for yourself, your family, and your business family. I know you are not the kind of person who will leave this future to chance. You are ready for this next big step in your business life.

Let's summarize the Saleability Blueprint:

If you want to increase the certainty that you will be able to sell your company when you want, for what you want, then you need to unpack these secrets:

1. Start one to seven years before you want to sell. Recognize that, depending on the number of red flags you have to fix and the time it takes to stabilize and then add green lights into your growth strategy, it may take two to four years to make a business saleable.

2. Commit to learning all you can about the process.

3. Invite partners, family, and stakeholders to learn about the process from you, or with you.

4. Explain the steps involved in building the Saleability Blueprint from Step 1 – Handle Reality through Step 4 – Helm the Transition.

5. Recognize that you will need advisors for every step. This is not a solo journey. Invite your accountant (audited books), lawyer (paper trail), exit planner, and coach into your planning process early on.

6. Explore the questions and come to terms with the answers (that work for everyone) for the five critical

questions that will determine when you exit, for how much, what your next act will be, the legacy that you want to leave, and the level of commitment all partners will give to making the business saleable.

7.   Build your custom Saleability Blueprint for all four steps so you know what to do and when to do it.

8.   Learn where to place your focus in your business in order to implement your plan to find and fix red flags (stabilization, which makes your company more profitable in the meantime), and then add green lights (growth strategies). Make the changes in your business to become what your buyer looks for.

9.   Find, hire, and mentor a leader to become your functional replacement.

10.   Mentor your management team as they grow your company.

Do all this, and then you're ready for a business broker or M&A advisor to get the deal done for you.

Chapter 8 Summary

These are the takeaways that we covered in this chapter. Which ones are you still unsure about? You may want to consider re-reading the chapters that focus on those parts of the plan that need more time to think through.

•   Following a Saleability Blueprint works even when you have multiple owners with different interests.

•   It takes dedication and commitment to make the

changes inside the business and a management team that you mentor so they can lead the next stage of growth.

- Follow the steps. Get the advice. Invest in your future. Skipping any of these steps makes the result you want take far longer to happen.

CHAPTER 9

HOW TO GET STARTED

To start this journey, you need to build your own Saleability Blueprint.

To build your plan, build on the momentum you've started just by reading this book. We invite you to:

Get Started Now So Your Company is More Profitable For You and Ready When Your Ideal Buyer Comes to Call

I want you to get the financial future and fine legacy that all your hard work and dedication deserves. Why? Because I care about our economy and don't want to see anyone's fortunes go down the drain. It's happening already. Please do us all a favor, and don't let it happen to you and your community. To get the future you really want with millions in your bank account rather than regrets in your heart, build your Saleability Blueprint so you are taking the right actions that serve your goals. All you need in order to do that is to get the *Make Your Business Saleable Resource System.*

This is an easy-to-follow, self-guided program. You will have everything you need to lead you, your family, and your partners to make the right decisions and right changes for your life, your legacy, your employees, and your company.

Here's what's inside:

1.   Three Critical Decisions DVD Series

A DVD series on how to make the three critical decisions that start you on the road to making your business saleable.

2.   *Fast-Track Secrets for Making Your Business Saleable* book and playbook by Lorraine and Rob McGregor

This is the textbook and playbook for our proven four-step system that you just learned about in this book. In it, we go deeply into demystifying all the complex issues so that you understand how buyers think, what will make your company more profitable, and what will make them search out your business over your competitors so that you can attract a premium offer. When you have read the book and researched, explored, and answered all the questions in the playbook, you will have a Saleability Blueprint that will guide you in what changes to make in order to become saleable.

3.   Exit Expert Interviews DVD Series

A DVD series of nineteen interviews with all the advisors you would normally have to find and consult with on your own, conveniently assembled in one location. Each advisor addresses a critical element in the all important "how to" become saleable process. You will: learn from the buyers themselves what it's like to work with an intermediary; hear from an owner on what he wished he knew before attempting to sell his business; understand how to get management buyout financing if you want to sell to family or employees; learn how to discover your next act; learn where the landmines are that sink a deal; and see how to navigate through this big life transition. Learning from these experts is like hiring nineteen $300-per-hour advisors to be on your team to help you fast-track your decision-making and planning process. The *Make Your Business Saleable Resource System* includes bound transcripts of all interviews.

This comprehensive series provides business owners and their financial advisors with critical perspectives never revealed before from how buyers evaluate businesses to the steps in an exit planning process.

You will hear from exit planners, transition coaches, business owners who tried to sell and failed, M&A professionals, lawyers, financial planners, wealth managers, family business experts, business brokers, strategic buyers, management buyout lenders, and private equity search specialists.

It would cost you thousands of dollars to find and hire the experts who have all this knowledge. We have done the work for you and brought them together so that you can learn from the comfort of your home or office. Remember, when you make your business saleable, you are making it more profitable now for you, the primary investor. Don't spend thousands trying to learn how to do this by yourself. Instead, you can buy the *Make Your Business Saleable Resource System* for $697.00 and save yourself time and money. To order the program, go to www.Spirit-West.com/Products. Don't let another year of profit uncertainty sit on your shoulders. We've got a surprise for you when you place your order. You'll also get instant access to our latest report, *6 Steps to Becoming a Profitable Go-To Business*. It's our gift to you for taking action. And you get a complementary phone call with us to help you get started. Because when we get a new book or idea we all have the best of intentions of starting it. And then life happens. We've got you covered on that too. We'll talk and help you move toward the future you really want.

Our 100% Money Back Guarantee

So, I imagine some of you are thinking about whether the Make

Your Business Saleable Resource System will be worth it. Well, I don't want you to worry about that. In our business, we live and breathe on being of value.

So, I'm going to give you this 60-day guarantee:

We will refund 100% of your money if you get to the end of the book, playbook, Three Critical Decisions DVD, and the nineteen Expert Interviews and feel you haven't learned anything you didn't know. Within sixty days, if you didn't see the value and you feel like it just didn't help you progress in building your Saleability Blueprint, then contact us at 206-395-3530 or here http://www.spiritwest.com/contact-us/, and we'll refund 100% of your money – no questions, no awkward conversations. We want you to feel ready to take the right action for you.

We look forward to being able to help you get started on your journey.

If you would like to order multiple copies of this book, "How to Increase the Value of Your Business Before You Sell… and Make It More Profitable Now!" for your clients, partners, and family members who need to understand what the journey to a successful exit looks like, then please visit our website at www.SpiritWest.com/Products.

GROUP MENTORING PROGRAM

Working through the building and implementation of a Saleability Blueprint can be fast tracked when you work with other owners in an environment that allows you to focus on this plan. If you want to accelerate your progress and work with the experts then call us and we'll tell you if we have a group starting in your area. 206-395-3530.

DO YOU HAVE BUSINESS PARTNERS?

Your partners and family members need to know how a business becomes saleable so that you can all work together. That alignment is essential for success. Make sure you order a copy of this book for everyone that has a stake in getting your business a premium exit.

REMEMBER: You can order all our products online at http://www.spiritwest.com/products. **Shipping is free.** You will receive your shipment in 5 - 7 days within the U.S. and 2 - 3 weeks internationally.

Thank you for taking the time to read this book.

I wish you a saleable business so you can claim your wealth when you want to by selling your business for the value you want because you have made it worth that number. This is how you will leave a legacy that counts. You can do this. It's your time.

CPSIA information can be obtained at www.ICGtesting.com
Printed in the USA
LVOW06*1804060714

393082LV00002B/33/P